D0006020

Que® Quick Reference Series

C Quick Reference

Alan C. Plantz

Que Corporation
Carmel, Indiana

Library of Congress Catalog Number: 88-61935

ISBN 0-88022-372-3

92 91 90   9 8 7 6

Interpretation of the printing code: the rightmost
double-digit number is the year of the book's printing;
the rightmost single-digit number, the number of the
book's printing. For example, a printing code of 88-4
shows that the fourth printing of the book occurred in
1988.

This book is based on Microsoft C 5.0, Microsoft
QuickC 1.0, Ecosoft C 4.0, Turbo C 1.5, and Lattice C
3.1.

Que Quick Reference Series

The *Que Quick Reference Series* is a portable resource of essential microcomputer knowledge. Whether you are a new or experienced user, you can rely on the high-quality information contained in these convenient guides.

Drawing on the experience of many of Que's best-selling authors, the *Que Quick Reference Series* helps you easily access important program information. Now it's easy to look up programming information for C and QuickBASIC 4, as well as often-used commands and functions for 1 2 3, WordPerfect 5, MS-DOS, and dBASE IV.

Use the *Que Quick Reference Series* as a compact alternative to confusing and complicated traditional documentation.

The *Que Quick Reference Series* also includes these titles:

> *QuickBASIC Quick Reference*
> *MS-DOS Quick Reference*
> *1-2-3 Quick Reference*
> *WordPerfect Quick Reference*

Publishing Manager
Allen L. Wyatt, Sr.

Product Directors
Karen A. Bluestein
Bill Nolan

Editors
Gregory S. Croy
Rebecca Kenyon

Editorial Assistant
Ann Taylor

Technical Editor
Scott Parker

Table of Contents

Trademark Acknowledgments

Que Corporation has made every effort to supply trademark information about company names, products, and services mentioned in this book. Trademarks indicated below were derived from various sources. Que Corporation cannot attest to the accuracy of this information.

ANSI is a registered trademark of American National Standards Institute.

Eco-C Compiler is a trademark of Ecosoft, Inc.

IBM is a registered trademark of International Business Machines Corporation.

LATTICE C COMPILER is a registered trademark of Lattice, Inc.

Microsoft C Compiler and MS-DOS are registered trademarks of Microsoft Corporation.

Turbo C is a registered trademark of Borland/ Analytica, International, Inc.

UNIX is a trademark of American Telephone and Telegraph Company.

VAX is a trademark of Digital Equipment Corporation.

Introduction

The C language, as created by Dennis M. Ritchie and fostered by Brian W. Kernighan, is one of the most popular computer languages available today. For several years now, C standards committee X3J11 of the American National Standards Institute (ANSI®) has been working to define stringently the C language. The result of their labors is *Programming Language C*—the ANSI C draft standard that preserves C's original form as much as possible yet adds functionality not present in its original form. Presently, the ANSI C draft standard has not been finalized, but this is expected shortly.

This book is intended to serve as a guide on how "ANSI C" is used on IBM® PC-compatible computers. The popular C compilers discussed in this book include:

❑ Turbo C® 1.5 by Borland/Analytica International, Inc.

❑ Microsoft® C 5.0 by Microsoft Corporation

❑ Microsoft QuickC® 1.0 by Microsoft Corporation

❑ LATTICE® C 3.1 by Lattice, Inc.

❑ Eco-C™ 4.0 by Ecosoft Inc.

among others, which vary in their degree of conformity with the ANSI C draft standard. Be aware that other compilers either recently have or are upgrading to comply with the ANSI report. Many machine-specific functions, such as those covering directories, graphics, and so on, are not covered in *C Quick Reference* because they are not part of the ANSI C draft standard. Code examples have been prepared using Turbo C 1.5.

There are other books that more fully explain the C language according to its "rebirth" as ANSI C, several of them published by Que Corporation:

❑ *C Programming Guide*, 2nd Edition

❑ *C Programmer's Library*

❑ *C Standard Library*

Data Types and Variables

All variables in C are declared or defined before they are used. A *declaration* indicates the type of a variable. If the declaration also causes storage to be set aside for the variable, it is a *definition*.

Data types in C are either *basic* or *complex* (composed of one part or many), and new types can be formed from the original types.

Declaring and Defining Variables

A variable declaration consists of a type specifier followed by the names of one or more variables of that type. Multiple variable names are separated by commas. The declarations

```
int x;
char yesno, ok;
```

declare x as a variable of type int, and yesno and ok as variables of type char.

Each variable name can be followed by an optional initialization expression:

```
int ordered = 1, onhand = 0;
float total = 43.132;
char *cptr  = NULL;
```

The variables ordered and onhand are initialized to values of 1 and 0, respectively, total is initialized to 43.132, and cptr is initialized to constant value NULL (0).

Basic Data Types

Table 1 gives the basic data types for C, their ranges, and their sizes. The char, int, short, and long types may be either signed or unsigned.

Table 1. C Data Types, Ranges, and Sizes

Type	_Range_	_Size in Bytes_
char (signed)	-128 to +127	1
char (unsigned)	0 to +255	1
enum	-32,768 to +32,767	2
int (signed)	-32,768 to +32,767	2
int (unsigned)	0 to +65,535	2
short (signed)	-32,768 to +32,767	2
short (unsigned)	0 to +65,535	2
long (signed)	-2,147,483,648 to +2,147,483,647	4
long (unsigned)	0 to +4,294,967,295	4
float	3.4E-38 to 3.4E+38	4
double	1.7E-308 to 1.7E+308	8
long double	1.7E-308 to 1.7E+308	8
pointer (near)		2
pointer (far, huge)		4

char

The char type is used to represent characters or integral values in a limited range (-128 to 127 or 0 to 255). Constants of type char can be characters enclosed in single quotation marks ('A','x'). Nonprinting characters (tab, formfeed, etc.) can be represented conveniently with escape sequences ('\t','\f'). For example:

```
char fstline;
static char drive = 'B';
```

The backslash (\) introduces an escape sequence. The standard escape sequences are shown in the following list. Note that the escape sequence for a single backslash is a double backslash (\\).

\a	Alert (bell) character
\b	Backspace
\f	Formfeed
\n	Newline (CR/LF pair)

\r	Carriage return (CR)
\t	Tab (horizontal)
\v	Tab (vertical)
\\	Backslash
\?	Question mark
\'	Single quotation mark
\"	Double quotation mark
\nnn	Octal number
\xnn	Hexadecimal number
'\0'	Null character (string terminator)

int, short, and long

These types represent integers (whole numbers) in C. The `short` and `int` types are the same in all micro-computer implementations of C. The size of an `int` can vary from computer to computer, but `short` is always two bytes and `long` is always four bytes.

Constants for integers can be:

❑ decimal, such as 3, 111, or 43859876

❑ octal, which are prefixed by 0, as in 012 (=10 decimal) or 076 (=62 decimal)

❑ hexadecimal, which are prefixed by 0x or 0X, such as 0x12 (=18 decimal) or 0x2f (=47 decimal)

Long integer constants use I or L as a suffix: 012L or 0x12L. The suffix U may be used by some compilers (Turbo C, for example) to indicate an unsigned constant. Integers can be declared and initialized, as in these examples:

```
int noOfBooks;
static short noOfPages;
static short namelen = strlen(name);
long recsUsed = 832198;
```

float and double

The `float` and `double` types apply to decimal numbers. The `float` type has 6 significant digits, while the `double` type has at least 10 significant digits. The IEEE floating point standard, followed by most C compilers, specifies 15 digits of precision for `double` and 18 digits of precision for `long double`.

3.14159, 1.3E-75, and -812.92 are all examples of floating point constants. Examples of floating point variables include the following:

```
float aveTime;
static float distance=483.71;
double lightyears=56.3819c7;
```

enum

The `enum` type is an "ordered list" of items as integer constants. Unless specified otherwise, the first member of an enumerated set of values has the value of 0, but you can also specify values. The declaration

```
enum weekdays {Sun, Mon, Tue, Wed,
      Thu, Fri, Sat}
```

means that Sun = 0, Mon = 1, etc. However, if you use

```
enum weekdays {Sun, Mon, Tue = 10,
      Wed, Thu, Fri, Sat}
```

then Sunday still equals 0, and Monday still equals 1; but now Tuesday equals 10, Wednesday equals 11, etc.

An enumerated type can be used to declare a variable:

```
enum weekdays anyday;
```

then used with

```
anyday = Tue;
```

Pointers

A pointer holds the address of another variable. It is declared by using an asterisk (*) in front of a variable name, as in

```
float *wirelen;
char *index;
```

A pointer can be assigned the address of a variable by using the address operator (&) before the variable name:

```
wirelen = &wire2;
```

The indirection operator (also an asterisk) is used to access the value in the address contained in a pointer. For example,

```
*wirelen = 30.5;
```

assigns the value 30.5 to the float variable pointed to by wirelen. This statement has the same effect as

```
wire2 = 30.5;
```

See the section "Type Qualifiers" and "Memory Models" for more information on pointers. See the section "Operators and Expressions" for further discussion of the * and & operators.

Variables in C have lvalues and rvalues. An lvalue, or left value, is the address of the variable. An rvalue, or right value, is the content of the variable. In other words, a pointer is used to get the rvalue of a variable by using the indirection operator.

Initializing Pointers

Pointers must be initialized by assigning an address. Any pointer can be initialized by following these steps:

1. Use a memory-allocation function such as malloc or calloc to create storage for a pointer:

```
intptr = (int*)malloc
        (sizeof(int));
```

2. Assign an existing variable's address to the pointer:

```
int funcresult;
intptr = &funcresult;
```

Pointers to strings are initialized by assigning the string to the pointer variable. If a string pointer is declared as `char *strptr;`, then the following assigns the string to the pointer:

```
strptr = "Enter a whole number: ";
```

Pointers and Arrays

If a program declares

```
float *arrayptr;
float farray[30]);
```

then `arrayptr` can be assigned the address of the beginning (the first element) of `farray` by using either of the following:

```
arrayptr = farray;
arrayptr = &farray[0];
```

No `&` (address operator) is needed when using the array name because compilers evaluate the name as an address automatically. However, the address operator is required when referring to an individual element in an array.

The name `farray[3]` also could be written as `*(farray + 3)` because the compiler converts it to this form.

Note: Pointers are variables and can be incremented and decremented (for example, `++arrayptr`). This cannot be done to an array because the array name is a constant address (for example, `farray++` is illegal).

Pointer arithmetic is adjusted for the size of the object pointed to. In the previous example of an array of `float`, the pointer will move `sizeof(float)`, or four bytes, as it is incremented or decremented. *Pointer arithmetic* involves the following:

❑ Assigning pointers of the same type.

❑ Assigning a pointer or comparing it to 0.

❑ Incrementing or decrementing a pointer.

❑ Adding, subtracting, or comparing pointers to members of an array.

❑ Relational and equality tests along with logical AND and OR.

❑ Addition or subtraction of integers.

❑ Converting from other pointer types or converting to and from integers.

Pointers to Pointers

Pointers can point to other pointers (called "double indirection"):

```
char **fstvar:
```

declares a pointer to another character pointer.

A pointer to a pointer can be used to access any element in an array. Because a pointer assigned to the name of an array accesses the beginning of the array (`arrayptr = farray;`), then using `*(arrayptr + 3)` would access the first element of the fourth row of the array (array subscripts start with 0).

The expression `char *argv[]` declares an array of character pointers to command-line arguments. An equivalent expression, using double indirection, is `char **argv`. A new command-line argument can be obtained by incrementing the pointer: `argv++`.

Pointers to Functions

Pointers can point to functions. The declaration

```
int (*ptrtofunction)(void);
```

creates a pointer to a function that returns an integer. A pointer can be assigned the address of a function by using the function name without any parameters:

```
ptrtofunction = calcdiff;
```

void

Void is a special type that is valueless. It has three distinct uses (also see the section "Keywords"):

1. The `void` type is used as a generic pointer without a type and can be used with any other type pointer:

   ```
   void *dummyptr;
   ```

   Earlier versions of C usually used a character pointer as a "generic" pointer.

2. The `void` type can be used to signify an empty parameter list:

   ```
   int sumtotals(void);
   ```

3. The `void` type is used as the return type of a function that does not return a value:

   ```
   void writedit(introw, intcol);
   ```

Complex or Aggregate Data Types

C's complex types include *arrays* (which include "strings" or arrays of characters), *structures*, *unions*, and *bitfields*.

Arrays

An array is a block of consecutive data items of the same type, referenced with a subscript. All arrays in C start with the subscript [0]. For instance, the single-dimensional array specified in

```
int grades[30];
```

is capable of storing 30 individual grades, grades[0] through grades[29]. A two-dimensional array such as

```
float weights[10][12];
```

would allocate storage for a total of 120 values. Other dimensions are added by adding another set of brackets.

In a nondefining declaration, such as in another source module or any place where no storage has been set aside by the compiler, a multidimensional array could be declared without specifying the size of the first dimension, as in

```
extern double dist[][10];
```

The size is obtained by the compiler from the original declaration.

The number of elements (members) of an array can be determined by dividing the size of the entire array by the size of one of the elements, as shown in this formula:

```
noofelements = sizeof(arrayname)
      / sizeof(arrayname[0])
```

This is often specified as a #define statement.

Static and Auto Arrays

A static array can be initialized when it is declared with

```
static char progerr[] =
      "Disk door not closed.";
```

An auto array can be initialized only with a constant expression in ANSI C. (See the section "Storage Class Modifiers" for information on static and auto arrays.) For example:

```
int smallmatrix[2][2] = {{32, 2},
      {95, 70}};
```

If not all members are assigned a value, they are
initialized to 0 by the compiler.

Arrays of Pointers

An array of pointers to characters can be initialized and
used like any other array as follows:

```
char *colors[] = {"magenta", "red",
        "mauve", "orchid", "rose"};
printf("colors = %s\n",
        colors[3]);
```

This would display

```
colors = orchid
```

Strings

Strings are simply character arrays (for example, `char
anystr[30]`), although they often are used in
connection with character pointers. Strings are always
terminated with a null value (`'\0'`) in C. String literals
(constants) may extend over two lines without special
punctuation, according to the ANSI standard, and will be
merged together:

```
char msg[] = "These two lines "
        "will be one.";
```

yields

```
"These two lines will be one."
```

Array declarations need not always specify the size of a
dimension (except the last one) because the compiler
can determine size. The statement

```
char fruitnames[][10] =
        {"orange", "banana", "apple"};
```

is interpreted by the compiler (for allocating storage) as
an effective declaration of

```
char fruitnames[3][10];
```

Structures

Structures (structs) are collections of data—often of different types—that can be acted upon as a whole. A structure can hold simple data types, such as characters, floats, arrays, and enumerated types. A structure also can hold types such as other structures, arrays, or unions. For example:

```
struct book {
    char title[50];
    char author[30];
    int pages;
    int pubyear;
};
```

A variable could be declared by using

```
struct book mybook;
```

To initialize and use the variable mybook, do the following:

```
struct book mybook = {"Debugging C",
                      "Robert Ward",
                      349, 1986};
```

To assign a specific value to the variable, use:

```
mybook.pages = 219;
```

Pointers to structures can also be made:

```
struct bookref *bookptr;
```

which would be used when referring to member:

```
bookptr->pages = 219;
```

(see also the "Operators and Expressions" section of this book.)

Many compilers now allow structures to be passed "en masse" to functions, allow structures to be returned by functions, and may even allow an entire structure to be assigned to another structure without having to do it member-by-member. You cannot, however, compare two structures to see if they are equal.

Structures may not contain structures of the same type, but they may contain pointers to structures of the same type. This example is wrong:

```
struct book {
    char title[50];
    char author[30];
    int pages;
    int pubyear;
    struct book abook;    /*WRONG*/
};
```

But this structure *could* contain a pointer to the structure:

```
struct book *bookptr;
```

Unions

Unions are almost identical to structures in their syntax. Unions provide a method of storing more than one type (although only one is used at any given time) at one memory location. A union definition causes enough storage to be reserved for the largest member. The declaration

```
union numtype {
    short anint;
    long  along;
    float afloat;
};
```

followed by the definition

```
union numtype numbertype;
```

causes four bytes (the size of a `float`) to be set aside for the variable `numbertype`.

The variable could then be assigned values in either of the following manners:

```
numbertype.anint = 341;
numbertype.along = 5882094
```

and so on. The preceding union could be initialized as:

```
union numtype { short anint; long
       along; float afloat; } = {57};
```

This form may vary and may not be supported by some compilers.

Bitfields

Bitfields often are used to put integers into spaces smaller than the compiler normally would use and are thus implementation-dependent. The compiler controls attributes such as the ordering of bits, whether unsigned or signed integers can be used, and so on. A bitfield always is specified within a structure by using a colon after the integer declaration along with the number of bits to be used (usually from 1 to 16). For example:

```
struct sample {
   int fstfield:4;
   short sndfield:6;
};
```

This sets up a member called fstfield where an integer will be fitted into four bits, and a second member called sndfield where the integer will be fitted into six bits.

Storage Class Modifiers

These modifiers are used to change the way a C compiler allocates storage for variables. extern, static, and typedef may be used with both variables and functions.

auto

auto indicates that a variable is automatic or local (restricted) in scope. This means the variable comes into being within the current block and does not exist after execution leaves the block. auto is permitted only in the heads of program blocks. Because auto is the default modifier, it is rarely seen.

extern

extern indicates a variable or function that is static in scope and is declared outside the module. A common use of an extern is to share data globally between two or more files.

register

register tells the compiler to place (if possible) the variable into the machine registers. This modifier is used to improve a program's speed and efficiency.

register is usually restricted for use with char and int variables and their pointers. You cannot use the & operator with register variables. Also, register normally is *not* used with function parameters. It is better programming style to declare local register variables within the routine and assign the parameters to them.

static

static may modify either variables or functions. It tells the compiler that the variable or function should be kept for the duration of the program from the point of declaration—even when going into other modules. A `static` variable retains its previous value from one function call to another.

=| typedef |=

`typedef` normally is used when defining variables or functions and means a new type is being formed. (Actually, you can rename only an existing type.)

`typedef` allows levels of data abstraction and makes for greater program clarity. If a variable were defined as

```
typedef struct BOOK;
```

then, instead of using

```
struct book mybook;
```

to declare a variable, you could use

```
BOOK mybook;
```

Another example is:

```
typedef char *STRING;
```

where you then can use the following declaration:

```
STRING booktitle;
```

in place of

```
char *booktitle;
```

This at least hides the fact you are using a `struct` as the underlying data type. Using typedefs also can aid portability; only the `typedef` need be changed instead of each statement using the new type.

Type Qualifiers

Type qualifiers define additional qualities of types besides storage and describe the "stability" of a variable. They may be used by themselves or with other type specifiers.

const

const is a new modifier from the ANSI standard.
const signals to the compiler that this variable's value
cannot be changed during the program by things such as
side effects, incrementing, and decrementing. A const
pointer cannot be changed even though the object it
points to could be changed.

Note: There is a difference between specifying

A. a variable (changing) pointer that points to a
   constant (nonchanging) object, such as

```
const char *ptr_to_const;
```

and specifying

B. a constant (nonchanging) pointer that points to a
   variable (changing) object, such as

```
char *const const_ptr;
```

In other words, in A, the value, or address, of the
pointer may change, but not the value of the character
it points to. In B, the value, or address, of the pointer
should *not* change, but the value of the character to
which it points could change. const may be used by
itself without a type, in which case a type of int is
assumed.

volatile

volatile is the opposite of the const qualifier and
states the variable can be changed at any time, not only
by the program but also by interrupts or by other outside
factors—the real-time clock, for example. volatile
also may prevent the compiler from performing any op-
timizations on the variable because its value can be
changed so readily. volatile is a new ANSI modifier
also.

Scope and Variable Lifetime

Global variables and functions come into being at the beginning of the program and last until the end of it. Others exist only while certain sections of the program are active. The area of a program where a variable is active or visible is called the `scope` of that variable.

ANSI C defines four types of scope: *function prototype* (limited to labels for `goto` statements), *block*, *file*, and *function*. The variable may be visible to the entire program, to a group of source files, to a family of functions, to a single function, or to an individual block of code. (See also the section "Storage Class Modifiers.")

A variable is *defined* only once, and at that time storage is allocated to it. A variable is *declared* whenever it is referenced in another file, and no storage is set aside during a declaration. A variable is *initialized* by the compiler only once (if at all) during the program when variables are defined and allocated storage.

Complex types (union, struct, arrays) of type `auto` usually cannot be initialized by the compiler. It is good practice to initialize them yourself.

A variable should be defined in one file and initialized there. For example:

```
char anychar = 'k';
```

A variable can be referenced in a declaration with the word `extern` in another file (`extern char anychar`) and should not be initialized there. Arrays of type extern may have empty brackets. For example:

```
extern float beamWeights[];
```

Global variables are defined before and outside of `main()`. They exist from the beginning to the end of the program and are normally initialized to 0 by the compiler.

External variables are defined outside the current module and exist as do static variables; they are usually initialized to 0 by the compiler.

External static variables are static variables declared outside a function. They are active from that point to the end of the program. They retain their values throughout the program and are initialized to 0 by the compiler.

Static variables exist from definition to the end of the program and occur inside a function. They retain their values between function calls and are normally initialized to 0 by the compiler.

Auto variables exist only within the block where they were defined: within a function, a loop, or inside braces. They are not initialized.

Register variables have the same scope as auto variables.

Operators and Expressions

C has a powerful set of operators. Used well, they add to the language's expressiveness and efficiency. Used poorly, they lead to expressions that are difficult to read or give the wrong result.

Table 2 lists the operators for C. The table shows the operators grouped from highest to lowest precedence. Operators within a group have the same precedence and associativity.

Table 2. C Operator Precedence and Associativity

L = left-to-right associativity, R = right-to-left associativity

Operator	*Function*	*Assoc.*
( )	membership	L
[ ]	membership	L
.	membership	L
->	membership	L

Operator	*Function*	*Assoc.*
-	unary	R
+	unary	R
~	unary	R
!	unary	R
*	unary	R
&	unary	R
++	unary	R
--	unary	R
sizeof	unary	R
(type)	unary	R
*	multiplicative	L
/	multiplicative	L
%	multiplicative	L
+	additive	L
-	additive	L
<<	bitwise	L
>>	bitwise	L
<	relational	L
>	relational	L
<=	relational	L
>=	relational	L
==	equality	L
!=	equality	L
&	bitwise	L
^	bitwise	L
|	bitwise	L
&&	logical	L
||	logical	L
?:	conditional	R
=, *=, /=, %=, +=, -=, <<=, >>=, &=, ^=, |=	assignment	R
,	series	L

Expressions

An expression is a combination of operators (such as + and =) and operands (variables) that produces a value. An expression can be used in most places where variables are used. Operators cause an action to be performed on the operands.

In C, no guarantee is given as to the order in which operators and operands are evaluated except in the cases of || (logical OR), && (logical AND), ?: (ternary), and the series operator (,), which forces left-to-right evaluation.

Expressions can change a variable *indirectly* during expression evaluation. An example of one of these "side effects" is a function that changes the value of a global variable when the global variable is not passed as an argument to the function.

Precedence and Associativity

Operators are classified by their *precedence* (rank of evaluation). For example, in the expression

```
x * y / (sizeof(z) * 3)
```

the parentheses have the highest precedence. (sizeof(z) * 3) is evaluated first; the result of the sizeof() operator is multiplied by 3. The other multiplication and division operators are performed on the resulting value.

When two or more operators have the same precedence, *associativity* determines the order of evaluation. Associativity is the order in which operators are grouped with operands. When two operators have the same precedence, the compiler uses the one that would come first under the rules of associativity. There are two basic rules of associativity:

1. Every operator has an associated *direction*, and operators within a group have the same direction. If operators in an expression have the same precedence, the expression will be evaluated in the direction (left-to-right or right-to-left) dictated by the associativity of the operators.

2. Operators have higher precedence when used as postfix operators than as prefix operators.

In the previous example, the multiplication and division operators have the same precedence. Both operators have left to right associativity, so y is grouped with the multiplication operator, rather than the division operator. The quantity x * y is evaluated, then the result divided by (sizeof(z) * 3).

All operators in C are evaluated from left to right except for unary, conditional (ternary), and assignment operators, which are evaluated from right to left.

Using a simpler example:

```
intresult = subtot[1] + subtot[2]
      - shipping;
```

Here the brackets are evaluated first, and the compiler gets the array values for subtot. Because the + and − operators have equal precedence and are evaluated from left to right, the two subtotals are added together, and then the shipping amount is subtracted. This would be the same as if parentheses had been used around the addition expression. For example:

```
intresult = (subtot[1] +
      subtot[2]) - shipping;
```

In expressions using operators with right-to-left associativity, such as:

```
dist = interval *= n;
```

the operand interval is grouped with the operator (*=) on its right, so (interval *= n) is evaluated and then assigned to dist.

Because expressions can be used in place of variables, statements such as the following could be used (although this is not done frequently because readability and "understandability" are reduced):

```
beginpoint = 1;
fststr = "programming";
sndstr = "programming";
intvalue == (beginpoint > 3,
      (strcmp(fststr, sndstr)
       == 0));
```

Here, the two parts of the last expression are evaluated, and then the result of the last part is assigned to intvalue. In the example, beginpoint > 3 is evaluated as either 0 or 1; and because either value is less than 3, the expression returns 0 (false). The strcmp is then done to comapre fststr and sndstr; and because the result of strcmp is equal to 0, a 1 (true) is returned, and the end value of intvalue equals 1.

According to the second rule for associativity, postfix operators have a higher precedence than prefix operators. If you are using the expression

```
arrayelement = *arraypointer++;
```

the pointer is incremented before the indirection operator is applied.

Operators

This section describes the C operators and their functions. These operators provide a rich variety of possible expressions.

Table 2 displays the operators in C arranged from highest to lowest precedence by group. The direction of associativity for each is indicated (L for left-to-right; R for right-to-left). The major groups of operators are membership, unary, arithmetic, bitwise shift, relational, equality, bitwise logical, logical, conditional (ternary), assignment, and series operators.

There are four general types of operators, depending on the number of operands required. *Unary operators* require one operand. *Binary operators* (arithmetic, bitwise, relational, equality, logical, assignment, and series operators) require two operands. There is only one *ternary operator*, the conditional operator, and it uses three operands. Membership operators are classified as "postfix expressions" along with the postfix increment (++) and postfix decrement (--) operators. A postfix expression means the operator occurs after the expression. See table 2 for the specific operators within each type.

In C, a symbol used as an operatory, such as the ampersand (&), can mean more than one thing. For instance, the ampersand may be used as the address operator (&studentscore), the bitwise AND operator (equipbyte & bytemask), or the logical AND operator ((begin == 1) && (num < 5)).

Another example is the asterisk (*), which may signify a pointer in a variable declaration, the indirection operator, or the multiplication operator.

Membership Operators

There are four *membership operators:* parentheses (), brackets [], dot (.) and arrow (->).

Membership operators in C are used with complex data types, such as functions, structures, and arrays. They can be used in conjunction with other operators like the indirection and address operators to provide complex expressions for obtaining a particular data item.

As an example, consider finding the 29th element of the 5th row in an array of doubles (stugr, or "student grade") where the element is a member of a structure (stustr). This structure is the 4th member of an array of structures (studata). The array of structures is also referenced by an array of pointers (stunun).

```c
#include <stdio.h>
void main(void)
{
    int i;
    double gr;
    typedef struct stu {
        char *stuname;
        double stugr[5][30];
    } stustr;

    /* define arrays */
    static stustr studata[10],
            *stunum[10];

    /* assign ptrs to array */
    for (i = 0; i < 10; i++ )
        stunum[i] = &studata[i];

    studata[3].stugr[4][28] = 3.25;

    /* print out 5 values */

    for (i = 0 ; i < 5; i++ ) {
        gr = stunum[i]->stugr[4][28];
        printf("Student %1d has a "
                "grade = %1.3f\n",
                i, gr);
    }
}
```

The output for all students other than `stunum[3]` is zero. The output for `stunum[3]` is 3.25. Note that data can be referenced through the pointer array rather than through the structure array by using the "arrow" operator and subscripts.

Specific information about the four membership operators follows.

Parentheses: () Parentheses are used in functions calls. For example:

```c
strcat(filename, fileext);
```

Brackets: [ ] Brackets enclose subscripts of arrays (and sometimes pointers) to indicate an individual array element. For example, the following expression refers to the second element in the fourth row of the array:

```
studentScores[3][1]
```

Dot: . The dot operator allows access to a "field" or structure member as in:

```
fileinfo.filename = inputfilename;
```

Arrow: -> The "arrow" operator (a hyphen and greater than sign) is used to reference a structure member by means of a pointer to the structure:

```
ptr->name = filename;
```

Unary Operators

The unary operators are those requiring only one operand and have a high level of precedence. The following paragraphs explain the unary operators.

Unary Minus: - The unary minus operator changes the sign of its operand. Unsigned operands produce unsigned results. The minus operator does not cause any change in the order of an expression's evaluation.

Unary Plus: + The unary plus operator returns the value of the operand. It also can be used to force the order of evaluation in an expression by telling the compiler not to rearrange the order of the expression to the right of the unary plus operator. This makes it act somewhat like a set of parentheses. The unary plus is a new operator in the ANSI standard.

One's Complement: ~ The one's complement operator, the tilde (~), inverts all bits within the affected variable (byte): 0's become 1's, and 1's become 0's.

Unary (Logical) Negation: ! The unary (logical) negation operator performs logical negation on its operand, so the result is true if the operand has a value of false, and false if the operand has a value of true. For example:

```
keepgoing = !done;
```

Indirection: `*` The indirection operator retrieves the value pointed to by a pointer. If `anystr` is a pointer to `string`, and

```
picturename = *anystr;
```

then `picturename` equals "Mona Lisa" if `anystr` pointed to a string variable containing that value. Alternatively, if you use

```
*anystr = "Mona Lisa";
```

you tell the compiler to assign the value "Mona Lisa" to the variable pointed to by `anystr`.

Address: `&` The address operator obtains the address of a variable or function. For example, if

```
anystr = &pict.title;
```

then `anystr` will contain the address of the variable `title` within the structure `pict`.

Increment/Decrement: `++/--` The increment operator (++) increases the value of a variable, and the decrement operator (--) decreases the value of a variable. They can be used either in front of (prefix) or behind (postfix) variables to give slightly different results. More information about using these operators is presented later in this section.

Sizeof: `sizeof()` This operator is not a function (which it resembles) but an actual operator in the C language. It returns the system size of an item:

```
sizeof(result)
```

If `result` is of type `integer`, the expression normally would return 2, and

```
sizeof(fileptr->filename)
```

where

```
filename = "OUT.TXT"
```

would return 7. You can use `sizeof()` to get the size of entire complex types, such as structures and unions.

Casts: (type) Cast operators transform variables or function results from one type to another. A cast is indicated by placing the desired type inside parentheses in front of the variable or function to be changed. For more information, see the section "Casts."

Increment and Decrement Operators Used with Variables

Given an integer variable `count` equal to 1, the expression `++count` means that `count` is incremented before being used (it is now 2) and then is used as in:

```
total += ++count;
```

If `total = 0` and `count = 1` before this statement, `count` is first incremented, then added to `total`; so `total = 2`, and `count = 2` after execution. On the other hand,

```
total += count++;
```

has a different result. `count++` means the value of `count` is used, then incremented. If `total = 0` and `count = 1` before this statement, `count` is added to `total`, then incremented; so `total = 1`, and `count = 2` after execution.

The same is true for the decrement operator. `--count` means that if `count = 2` before the statement, it would equal 1 before being used. In contrast, `count--` means if `count = 2` before the statement, it is used with the value of 2, and then decremented after the statement is executed.

Increment and Decrement Operators Used with Pointers

In the case of pointers, the increment and decrement operators work differently. Pointers are not necessarily changed by 1, but rather by the size of the type pointed to by the pointer.

For instance, if the pointer variable `intptr` points to an integer stored at address 1000, then after executing `++intptr`, the variable would point to address 1002, because the size of an integer is 2 bytes. Additionally, if a pointer points to a structure with a size of 415 bytes (at address 1000), then that pointer will be incremented by 415 bytes to address 1415.

If the pointer points to a float, as in `*(floatptr + 3) = 0.82;`, adding a value to the pointer means adding the size of three floats (12 bytes) to `floatptr` and not adding 3 bytes to `floatptr`. The general form is

```
pointer +/- (n * sizeof(what the
        pointer points to))
```

where the compiler adds or subtracts the quantity of `n` items multiplied by the size of the item's type.

Casts

Casts transform variables or function results from one type to another. A cast is indicated by placing the desired type inside parentheses in front of the variable or function to be changed. Consider the following:

```
float total;
float days;
int grandtotal;
grandtotal = total/days;
```

In this sequence, you are trying to put a `float` into an integer variable, and you get a compiler error. The cast

```
grandtotal = (int)total/days;
```

would solve the problem because the compiler is now told to convert the division result into an integer.

In another example, you could convert a variable into a type required by a function parameter for proper manipulation or as a return value. If you use the function

```
int wholeNoSum(int fstvalue,
        int sndvalue)
```

with the following example:

```
double subtotal1, subtotal2;
int result;
result = wholeNoSum((int)
      subtotal1, (int)subtotal2);
```

you must cast the parameters as integers so that they will be properly accepted by the function.

Arithmetic Operators

The arithmetic operators are *binary* operators and operate as in normal arithmetic expressions. The multiplicative operators (*, /, %) have higher precedence than the additive operators (+ and -).

Multiplication: * The multiplication operator multiplies two operands:

```
sum = value1 * value2;
```

Division: / The division operator produces the quotient of two operands:

```
result = value1 / value2
```

Modulus: % The modulus (remainder) operator returns the remainder of a division. If value1 equals 17 and value2 equals 5, then

```
result = value1 % value2;
```

puts the value of 2 into result (17 divided by 5 equals 3 plus a remainder of 2).

Addition: + The addition operator adds two operands.

Subtraction: - The subtraction operator subtracts one operand from another.

Bitwise Operators

Bit operators, which are usually binary operators, can be used only with characters or integers. They include & (AND), | (OR), ^ (XOR or exclusive OR), << (left shift) and >> (right shift). The one's complement operator (~) has been discussed previously under unary operators but is also considered a bitwise operator.

Binary operators vary in precedence. The one's complement operator comes first, followed by the left and right shifts, the bitwise AND, OR, and exclusive OR.

Left Shift/Right Shift: <</>> The shift operators move the bits in a byte a specified number of places. The syntax of the statement is:

```
variable = variable << or >> places;
```

Thus,

```
status = byte << 4;
```

places in status a value equal to byte shifted 4 places to the left.

Bitwise AND: & The bitwise AND operator returns a bit value of 1 if both bits it compares have values of 1; otherwise, it returns a value of 0.

Bitwise OR: | The bitwise inclusive OR operator returns a value of 1 if either bit it compares has a value of 1; otherwise, it returns a value of 0.

Bitwise XOR: ^ The bitwise exclusive OR operator (XOR) returns a value of 0 unless one bit has a value of 1 and the other bit compared has a value of 0.

Another use of the shift operators is for dividing or multiplying integral values by powers of 2. Shift operators are useful because they are more efficient than using the division and multiplication operators. This means that shifting an integer, such as 17, to the left by 3 is the same as $17 \times 8 = 136$.

Relational Operators

Expressions using the relational operators return either 0 (false) or 1 (true).

Less than: < The less than operator compares two values and returns a value of 1 if the first operand has a value less than that of the second operand; otherwise, 0 is returned.

Greater than: > The greater than operator compares two values and returns a value of 1 if the first operand has a value greater than that of the second operand; otherwise, 0 is returned.

Less than or equal to: <= The less than or equal to operator compares two values and returns a value of 1 if the first operand has a value less than or equal to that of the second operand; otherwise, 0 is returned.

Greater than or equal to: => The greater than or equal to operator compares two values and returns a value of 1 if the first operand has a value greater than or equal to that of the second operand; otherwise, 0 is returned.

Equality Operators

The equality operators (== and !=) stand for "is equal to" and "is not equal to," respectively. They require two operands and return either 0 (false) or 1 (true). Both operators are used to examine the relationships of their operands.

Equal: == The "equal" operator returns a value of 1 if the expression is true; otherwise, 0 is returned. If x = 3, then the expression (x == 3) is true. If, however, x = 93, then the test (x == 3) is false.

Not equal: != The "not equal" operator tests both its operands to see if the first is not equal to the second and returns 1 if true, or 0 if false.

Note the difference between the = and == operators. The = operator assigns; the == operator tests equality. If the variable `starttime` = 1 and the variable `begintime` = 2, then the statement

```
if (starttime = begintime)
    printf("Time to start\n");
```

means the value of `begintime` is assigned to `starttime`, so `starttime` now equals 2. The compiler sees this as "if (2)...", so the program prints "`Time to start`" because the `if` statement was true (not 0). If the expression were written

```
if (starttime == begintime)
    printf("Time to start\n");
```

then the compiler first checks to see if the values of `starttime` and `begintime` are equal. `starttime` =1, and `begintime` = 2, so they are not equal. The compiler, therefore, continues the same as if it were "if (0)...", and the statement "`Time to start`" is not printed. Both forms of the `if` statement are legal in C, so you must be careful to check this.

Logical Operators

Logical operators compare two expressions and return a value of 0 (false) or 1 (true). The logical AND has precedence over the logical OR. Logical operators are often used in `if...else` statements or loops where conditional expressions are allowed.

C allows the logical expressions to "short circuit." As soon as the result of an expression is known, evaluation stops. With the expression:

```
if (c == 'Y' || c == 'y')
```

if `c` has the value of `'Y'` (making the expression true), then the second part of the expression (`c == 'y'`) is not evaluated.

Logical AND: && The logical AND operator returns 0 and (because of "short-circuit" evaluation) does not evaluate the second part if the expression to the left of the operator is false; otherwise; 1 is returned.

Logical OR: || The logical OR operator returns 1 and (because of "short-circuit" evaluation) does not evaluate the second part if the expression to the left of the operator is true; otherwise, 0 is returned.

Conditional Operator

The conditional (or *ternary)* operator consists of the question mark and colon used together and requires three operands. It resembles an if...else clause in many ways and could result in more efficient code from the compiler. The following statement:

```
result = mode > 0 ? 1 : 0;
```

is read as:

```
if mode > 0 then result = 1
     else result = 0.
```

The conditional operator could also be used in a function return statement:

```
return(mode == finished ? 0 : 1);
```

which is read

```
if(mode == finished) then return(0)
     else return(1);
```

and causes 0 to be returned by the function if mode == finished; otherwise, 1 is returned.

Assignment Operators

The binary assignment operators are best thought of as "combined" operators. They are used to shorten expressions. For example, the expression:

```
total = total + amt;
```

repeats the variable `total`. C allows you to use the expression:

```
total += amt;
```

which means the same thing without repeating the second `total`. Simple assignment is provided by using the equal sign alone, and complex assignment is provided by using the equal sign combined with another operator.

`=`   The equal sign provides simple assignment of a value to the operand on the left of the = operator, so to assign the value of 3.14159 to a float, use `pivalue = 3.14159;`.

`*=`   The multiplication symbol and equal sign are used to express multiplying the left-hand operand by the right-hand operand and assigning the result back to the left-hand operand.

`/=`   The division symbol and equal sign are used to divide the left-hand operand by the right-hand operand and assign the resulting value to the operand on the left of the /= operator.

`%=`   The percent sign and equal sign make this binary assignment operator. The left-hand operand undergoes a modulus operation with the operand to the right of the %= operator, and the remainder is assigned back to the left-hand operand.

`+=`   The plus and equal signs form this operator. It assigns the resulting value to the left-hand operand after first adding the left-hand and right-hand operands together.

`-=`   The minus and equal signs form this operator. It assigns the resulting value to the left-hand operand after first subtracting the right-hand from the left-hand operand.

`<<=`   This operator consists of the left shift and equal operators. The left-hand operand is shifted to the left by the amount specified in the right-hand operand, and the result is assigned back to the operand on the left. For example:

```
byteval <<= 4;
```

`byteval` is shifted left 4 places, then the new value is assigned to `byteval`.

`>>=` This operator consists of the right shift and equal operators. The left-hand operand is shifted to the right by the amount specified in the right-hand operand, and the result is assigned back to the operand on the left.

`&=` The `&=` assignment operator provides a bitwise AND of the left-hand and right-hand operands and assigns the result to the left-hand operand.

`^=` The `^=` assignment operator provides a bitwise exclusive OR (XOR) of the left-hand and right-hand operands and assigns the result to the left-hand operand.

`|=` The `|=` assignment operator provides a bitwise inclusive OR of the left-hand and right-hand operands and assigns the result to the left-hand operand.

Series Operator (,)

The series operator, the comma, indicates a series of statements executed from left to right. It commonly is used in loops, particularly `for` statements. For instance:

```
for (i = 1; i < 10; ++i, ++j);
```

would cause not only the variable `i` but also the variable `j` to be incremented each time the loop is executed.

Data Type Conversion

Using operators, particularly casts or arithmetic operators, can cause changes in precision of values during data conversion. Some precision may be lost during conversion from larger to smaller data types, such as from `double` to `char`. Converting from a smaller to a larger type, such as from `char` to `float`, generally preserves both the precision and the sign of the values. Table 3 shows the result of common type conversion operations.

Table 3. Data Type Conversions

Original	*Converted*	*Result*
int, long	char	Uses low-order byte
float, double*	char	`float` or `double` becomes a `long`, then low-order byte is used
long	int	Two bytes (low-order) used
float, double*	int	`float` becomes `long`, then two least-significant bytes are used
float, double*	long	Integer portion is taken; not defined if too large to fit into long type

*In some compilers (Microsoft C, for example) the `double` first may be converted to a `float`, then from a `float` to the lower type, resulting in possibly more precision loss than those converting directly.

The C Preprocessor

The C preprocessor substitutes text, merges or pastes tokens, performs a conditional compilation, includes other files as part of the source, and signals compiler directives in the source code before the code is handed over to the compiler.

Substitutions may be in the form of a *macro*, in which a name is assigned to a value (in a macro's simplest form); the name can then be used throughout the program. The value assigned to a name can be changed in the #define statement without having to change it each time the name appears in the source. In another form, a macro can be the body of a function. If parameters are used, the compiler allows any data type to be used, so that routines such as sorting and comparing can become generic. Macros free the programmer from writing separate routines for integers, strings, and so on.

Another major task of the preprocessor is to allow *conditional compilation* in which sections of code are actually compiled or ignored, depending on whether conditions are true or false. Code for different environments or operating systems can be put into one source file and then compiled. Conditional preprocessor directives can then be used to determine which code is compiled.

The preprocessor usually can be run separately from the compiler. The output from it can be directed to a file or to the screen in order to view exactly what substitutions are taking place, which #define values are active, and so on.

Predefined Macros

ANSI C requires five macros in compatible implementations. All of them start and end with two underscores, so the macro has four underscores in all.

_ _LINE_ _	The line number of the source file currently being processed, with the first line starting with 1 (not supported in Eco-C).
_ _FILE_ _	The name of the source file currently being processed. It may encompass #include files and can be useful in error messages (not supported in Eco-C).

_ _DATE_ _	Contains the date that processing began on the source file in the form of mmm dd yyyy, for example, Feb 21 1988 (not supported in Microsoft C, LATTICE C, or Eco-C).
_ _TIME_ _	A string containing the time processing began on the source file, in the form hh:mm:ss. (not supported in Microsoft C, LATTICE C, or Eco-C).
_ _STDC_ _	A macro that is true (value of 1) if compiler conditions are set to denote ANSI C compatibility; otherwise, it is undefined (not supported in Microsoft C, LATTICE C, or Eco-C).

Compilers used on 8088/86 machines often have a number of other (non ANSI) predefined system-specific or compiler-specific macros.

_ _TURBOC_ _	Used by Turbo C to denote the Turbo C compiler is in use and which contains the compiler's version number (not supported in Microsoft C, LATTICE C, or Eco-C).
_ _PASCAL_ _	The same as a command-line option signaling Pascal conventions for identifiers and function parameters (not supported in Microsoft C, LATTICE C, or Eco-C).
_ _MSDOS_ _	Has the value of 1 for all compilers to denote the MS-DOS® operating system (not supported in Eco-C).
_ _CDECL_ _	Denotes C calling conventions are used instead of Pascal–usually the default condition (not supported in Microsoft C, LATTICE C, or Eco-C).

LINT_ARGS   Tells the compiler to use strong type-checking on functions (prototyping). Normally, two sets of function declarations are present in the header files, one with parameter types given to be used when LINT_ARG is defined, the other without (not supported in Turbo C or Eco-C).

M_I86   This macro is always defined and tells the compiler the machine is in the 80x86 family of processors (not supported in Turbo C, LATTICE C, or Eco-C).

NO_EXT_KEYS   This macro is active in Microsoft C only when the /Za compiler switch is given to disable special keywords of cdecl, far, fortran, huge, near, and pascal.

Directives

Preprocessor directives are discussed in the subsections that follow.

(null) Directive

The null directive, consisting of a # followed by a newline, does not cause any action to be performed. It can act as a "filler." An example of this usage would be to replace the body of a for loop when all of the action is specified by the three expressions governing conditions. For example:

```
for (i = 1; len < end; i++) {
#
}
```

This code increments i and does nothing else.

Directive

The ## directive creates the effect of "token pasting" in C. If the following is used:

```
#define STR(a)    str ## a
STR(1) = strcat(STR(2),
        STR(3));
```

the preprocessor merges or combines the token into:

```
str1 = strcat(str2, str3);
```

White space (tabs, spaces, etc.) around the ## directive is discarded.

#define Directives

#define directives are common in C and tell the compiler to substitute values for names during compilation. These directives have the general form:

```
#define <NAME> <substitution>
```

where NAME is usually in uppercase. The substitution may be a single value or something as elaborate as the entire body to a function. An example is:

```
#define BLACK 0
```

or

```
#define QC "QuickC"
```

Any time the term BLACK is found by the preprocessor, the value 0 is substituted. Likewise, whenever QC is found, "QuickC"— double quotation marks and all — is substituted. If a semicolon is placed after the statement, it also will be included (probably in error). If the #define value must be carried over to another line, then the backslash (\ ) character should be the last thing on the line to let the preprocessor know a continuation will occur.

Macros can be used to create "pseudo-functions." These functions are truly generic because data of any type can be used with them as long as the macro contains the proper statements. Some compilers may put limits on the size of function macro or on the number of parameters allowed. For example:

```
#define DOCALC(a,b) \
((a * b) + (a - 3) - \
(MAXINT - 71b))
```

could use integers (short, long, unsigned, etc.), floats, or doubles successfully.

#undef Directive

Tokens may be undefined by using `#undef <NAME>` as in `#undef BLACK`. This causes the preprocessor to act as if the token does not exist. The term may be later redefined in the source if desired.

#include Directive

Another file can be incorporated into a source file by means of the `#include` directive. It consists of

```
#include <filename>
```

where filename may or may not require the complete path to the file, for example, `#include <math.h>`. Usually, the compiler allows the user to set up certain standard directories where the system header files and libraries are located. Names of files in the standard directories are enclosed in angle brackets (< >). Files not in these directories are enclosed in quotation marks, and the compiler typically first searches the current default directory for these files unless a path is cited.

Conditional Compilation Directives

Conditional compilation allows certain sections of code to be compiled or executed depending on conditions stated in the code. For example, code may not be compiled if a particular memory model is used or if a value is undefined.

This family of directives includes #if, #ifdef, #ifndef, #endif, #else, and #elif. They are used basically the same as "if-then-else" statements. The #if family also can be nested and is used with the #define directives for setting conditions.

#elif is a new statement from ANSI C and is like a combination #else and #if statement. #elif simplifies nesting when many levels are used. Instead of writing:

```
#if condition1
    statement1;
#else
#if condition2
    statement2;
#else
    default;
#endif
#endif
```

the programmer can write:

```
#if condition1
    statement1;
#elif condition2
    statement2;
#else
    default;
#endif
```

Note that Turbo C allows the use of the `sizeof()` operator in conditional compilation statements. This is not supported by ANSI C and other compilers.

#ifdef and #ifndef

These statements allow testing within the preprocessor to see if a name has been defined. They also can ensure that a macro is defined if not done previously so that it cannot be overlooked. Using `#ifdef VAX` would be valid if the statement `#define VAX 1` preceded the `#ifdef` statement and is equivalent to `#if VAX`. `#ifndef` checks if a name has *not* been defined.

#if defined( )

This is not implemented by all compilers but is part of ANSI C, and the `defined` section is actually an operator. Using

```
#if defined(MSDOS)
```

is the same as using

```
#ifdef MSDOS
```

The major advantage is in allowing more complex expressions using `#if`:

```
#if defined(MSDOS) && defined(TC)
    printf("Now using Turbo C"
        "under MSDOS\n");
#endif
```

rather than

```
#ifdef MSDOS
#ifdef TC
    printf("Now using Turbo C "
            "under MSDOS\n");
#endif
#endif
```

#error

This new statement in the ANSI C standard produces a compile-time error message useful in debugging preprocessor directives when conditions are not met. For example:

```
#error "MSDOS not defined"
```

The preprocessor stops if the condition is not met, then displays the file name and line number where the error occurred along with the error message. This directive is supported only in Turbo C.

#line

The #line statement is of two forms.

```
#line <integer constant>
       [file name]
```

or

```
#line <integer constant>
```

commanding the compiler that the next source line corresponds to the line integer constant and possibly is found in file name (optional), as in #line 312 outtxt.c. It helps when source is produced from something other than the current implementation. This directive is supported only in Turbo C.

#pragma

This is an ANSI C statement that allows inclusion of compiler-specific information in the form:

```
#pragma <directive>
```

The ANSI standard states that each compiler specifies the directives it recognizes so that certain directives can

be set up by the compiler manufacturer without interfer-
ing with those from other manufacturers. For example,
Turbo C allows the two following directives:

```
#pragma inline
#pragma warn
```

Microsoft C allows three options:

```
#pragma pack
#pragma loop_opt
#pragma check_stack
```

to specify optimizing features.

Lattice C also allows #pragma statements.

Memory Models and Memory Management

Microcomputers that use the 8088 family of processors
let programmers choose among different memory
models to make their code more efficient. This chapter
discusses the different models and how to use them.

Segments

Personal computers with 8088/86/186/286 processors
have a *segmented architecture*. This means their
memory is not manipulated in one chunk but is divided
into 64K segments. Segments start on paragraph
boundaries (even multiples of 16). Addresses within a
segment start at 0 hex and go to FFFF hex.

To find a particular address within a segment (held in 16
bits), specify an offset (also held in 16 bits) after the
segment in the form of segment:offset. The
absolute address is calculated by shifting the segment
address left by 4 bits and then adding the offset address.
This calculation yields a 20-bit address value.

Registers

A segment address is loaded into the segment register and can be used by the program. Registers are hardware locations that hold and manipulate values. However, if you wish to gain access to a memory location outside of this segment, you must either load that segment's address into the register or get at it by using a 32-bit value. This address is calculated by shifting the segment address value left by 16 bits and then adding the offset.

Pointers

A `far` pointer is a 32-bit pointer that can access memory outside of the segment currently being used. A `near` pointer is only 16 bits (2 bytes) and accesses memory only within the current segment. It is the default pointer used by C.

Another kind of pointer, the `huge` pointer, is similar to the `far` pointer in size (32 bits), but is not subject to some problems that can occur with `far` pointers. A `huge` pointer can be formed by calculating the 20-bit address value, then using the leftmost 16 bits for the segment address value and the rightmost 4 bits for the offset.

The `huge` pointer has the same value or address after shifting and wraps around the value when you reach the top end of the register. For example, if the huge pointer is at 714D:0000, decrementing the pointer would shift it to 714C:000F. Likewise, a huge pointer at 714C:000F would hold the address 714D:0000 when incremented.

The `huge` pointer has a unique address different from all other huge pointers, so any confusion is eliminated. On the other hand, huge pointers are slower in operation because they require additional math to calculate the address values.

Memory Models

C compilers on 8086-family machines support different memory models. The compilers may restrict the size of a single data item, such as an array, in the large and huge models. Usually, as in the large model, the data item cannot be larger than 64K. In the huge model, however, the data item may be larger than 64K under certain circumstances, such as a requirement that no single element be larger than 64K.

Conversions may vary from compiler to compiler. Microsoft C handles conversions correctly. The Turbo C compiler does not accept a single data item larger than 64K (no single item can be larger than a segment within a single source module) when using the huge memory model. However, the data item may be allocated on the heap using a pointer of type huge. The heap is the remainder of memory from the top of the stack upwards, and is present in all memory models. Table 4 is a general guide to code, data, and pointer sizes in the various memory models.

Table 4. Memory Models for C Compilers

Model	Code Size	Data Size	Code Pointers	Data Pointers
Tiny	64K	64K	near	near
Small	64K	64K	near	near
Medium	1M	64K	near	far
Compact	64K	1M	far	near
Large	1M	1M	far	far
Huge	1M	1M	far	far

To choose one of the various memory models, you need to know the approximate amount of storage required for your code and data. From this information you can choose the appropriate memory model. You can "mix 'n' match" memory models by using one for the majority of your program (code and data), and then use the near, far, or huge modifiers with data objects or functions to access memory outside of the memory model in effect.

The special segment modifiers, which are `near` pointers, also come into play here. For example:

```
int _do *anyptr;
```

creates a pointer to type `int` into the data segment.

Mixing memory models is also an efficient use of program size. If you are using a small memory model (`tiny`, `small`, `medium`), then use the `far` or `huge` modifiers for data items or functions that would lie outside of the 64K limits. If you are using a large memory model (`compact`, `large`, `huge`), you can still use the `far` and `huge` modifiers for large items, but you can use also the `near` modifier for items small enough to fit within 64K if you want to increase access speed.

Note: Functions cannot be modified using `huge`. Remember that the memory model can be checked during compilation in Turbo C by using conditional compilation statements and the predefined macros (`_ _TINY_ _`, `_ _SMALL_ _`, etc.). This is also a method for defining whether to use certain pointer modifiers or segment modifiers.

File Input and Output in C

C provides two types of file input and output: standard (or high- level) I/O, and system (or low-level) I/O. The standard I/O functions are precisely defined in the ANSI standard, but the system I/O functions, being machine-specific, are not. Both standard and system I/O can be used to handle physical devices such as disks, terminals, MIDI ports, printers, etc.

C treats disk files and devices (printers, the console, and other peripherals) alike. Because most file I/O functions are device- independent, much of their usage is transparent. There may be certain physical limitations, however, such as reading a character from a printer, or "rewinding" the console. On the other hand, a device "file" can be opened, closed, and reassigned just like a disk file. Both standard and system-level routines should function on both disk files and devices.

Standard I/O and Streams

I/O devices in C are regarded as *streams* of bytes. Streams should behave the same on all systems, but files may not. Standard streams include stdout (standard output-terminal), stdin (standard input-keyboard), and stderr (standard error output-terminal). Other streams may be stdaux (standard auxiliary device-serial port) or stdprn (standard device-printer).

If I/O is buffered, the stream information is stored temporarily in a buffer. Buffering can be set with setbuf(), setvbuf(), or with the system constant BUFSIZE (in stdio.h). Buffering can be done a line at a time or a block at a time. The buffer is emptied (flushed) when it gets full, when the fflush() function is called, when the file is closed, or when the program ends.

A stream can be opened or created with fopen(). The function returns a pointer to the stream; a NULL value signifies an error.

fopen() opens the file using the mode provided. The default mode is text. Table 5 gives the symbols used to designate file modes.

Table 5. Symbols for File Modes

Symbol	File mode
r	read
w	write
a	append
rb	read (binary file)
wb	write (binary file)
ab	append (binary file)
r+, w+, a+	read or write
rb+, wb+, ab+	open for read/write (binary file)

A file can be opened in either text or binary mode. Text mode generally consists of data in the form of lines of characters that may have newlines at the end. Binary mode is a sequence of bytes rather than characters and represents data as it is stored in memory.

A file position indicator normally is set to position 0 (beginning of the file) when a file is opened. The function ftell() reports the current indicator position, and fseek() moves the indicator. Another function, rewind(), sets the file indicator to the beginning of the file.

When a file is opened, data can be read and written in text mode as an unformatted or formatted character or string or as a record using the functions in table 6.

Table 6. Stream Input/Output for Standard I/O

	Character	*String*	*Formatted*	*Record*
Read	fgetc()	fgets()	fscanf()	fread()
	getc()	gets()	scanf()	
Write	fputc()	fputs()	fprintf()	fwrite()
	putc()	puts()	printf()	

The end-of-line (a newline or ASCII decimal 10 character) in a standard C file is represented in DOS as a carriage-return/line-feed pair (ASCII decimal 13 and 10). In text files, the EOF character is usually an ASCII decimal 26 (Ctrl-Z). In binary files, EOF is determined by file length. The functions feof() and eof() can be used to detect this condition.

Errors can be detected with ferror() and perror(). They can be cleared with clearerr(). When processing is finished, a stream may be closed using fclose().

System I/O for Files

Low-level I/O involves using *file handles* (an integer value representing the file) instead of streams (pointers).

The same standard system files are available as handles, as shown in table 7.

Table 7. Standard File Handles

File	*Handle*
stdin	0
stdout	1
stderr	2
stdaux	3
stdprn	4

The data is not formatted or buffered by the system. Buffering can be done by the programmer by using variables, memory manipulation routines, and so on. The file can be opened using open (), which returns a handle if no problems occur. The file can also be subject to various modes of operation set by using flags, as shown in table 8.

Table 8. Flags for File Modes

Flag	*Significance*
O_APPEND	position file pointer at end of file
O_CREAT	create a new file
O_RDONLY	open for reading only
O_RDWR	use for both reading and writing
O_TRUNC	open an existing file and truncate it to a length of 0
O_WRONLY	open for writing only
O_BINARY	open in binary mode
O_TEXT	open in text mode
S_IWRITE	writing permitted
S_IREAD	reading permitted

If the O_CREAT flag is used, then the S_IWRITE and/or S_IREAD flags must also be used.

The read () function obtains information from the file, and write () puts data in the file. The function `tell()` returns the position of the file indicator, and `lseek()` can position the indicator at a particular location. Error conditions are detected with `perror()`. Use the routine `close()` to close the file properly.

Note: Do *not* mix standard and system file access when working with an open file.

Console and Port I/O

This portion of I/O is specific to MS-DOS. The `conio.h` header file contains declarations and prototypes. The routines specific to console and port I/O are summarized in table 9.

Table 9. Summary of Console and Port I/O

Function	Result
cgets()	Retrieves string from console
cscanf()	Retrieves data from console
getch()	Retrieves character from console
getche()	Retrieves character from console
ungetc()	Puts character back into keyboard buffer so that it can be reread
cprintf()	Displays data on-screen
cputs()	Displays a string on-screen
putch()	Displays a character on-screen
kbhit()	Checks keyboard buffer for keystrokes
inp()	Inputs to a port
outp()	Reads from a port

The console and port devices do not have to be opened or closed, unlike normal streams and files. They are not compatible with the standard or system level routines, so problems could occur if used in conjunction with them.

Keywords

Table 10 lists the keywords defined by the ANSI C standard and used by all C compilers. The table lists also some additional keywords reserved by microcomputer implementations of C compilers but not defined in the ANSI standard.

Table 10. C Keywords

ANSI Standard Keywords

auto	extern	sizeof
break	float	static
case	for	struct
char	goto	switch
const	if	typedef
continue	int	union
default	long	unsigned
do	register	void
double	return	volatile
else	short	while
enum	signed	

Additional Keywords for Microcomputers

asm	_es	interrupt
cdecl	far	near
_cs	fortran	pascal
_ds	huge	_ss

Note: Turbo C also has keywords corresponding to the IBM PC's registers, which appear in uppercase prefixed by an underscore (for example, _AH). All the preceding keywords (except fortran) are in Turbo C; Microsoft C uses cdecl, far, fortran, huge, near, and pascal. Lattice C uses the same as Microsoft except for fortran.

Keywords for Microcomputers

asm

Used by compilers such as Turbo C to denote the inclusion of in-line assembly code within routines. asm is of the form:

```
asm <opcode> <operands>
```

as in

```
asm push ds;
```

You may terminate the command line with either a semicolon or newline character. You may also need to use a command-line option or statement such as #pragma inline to use asm.

auto

The default storage class (local scope) for most function variables. The variable exists only for the duration of the block in which it is defined.

break

Used to exit unconditionally from a for, while, do...while loop, or from a case section of a switch statement. Within a switch statement, the break clause in a case section signals the compiler to quit executing any remaining case sections and exit the switch statement. For example:

```
for (i = 1; i < 255;
        ++i) {
    c = getchar();
    if (c == ESC) break;
    c = toupper(c);
    printf("%c", c);
}
```

case

A section (a specific match) within a `switch` statement. See `switch`.

cdecl

Compilers normally allow you to call routines in other languages. Indentifiers are used by the linker in their original form (uppercase, lowercase, or mixed) and are preceded with an underscore. The order in which function parameters are pushed onto and popped from the stack depends upon the language. C works from right to left; Pascal, from left to right. Use of the `cdecl` modifier in front of an identifier or function indicates that the normal C function-call conventions should be used instead of those of another language. See also the `pascal` modifier.

char

A simple variable type representing a single byte.

const

A modifier that means the variable's value cannot be changed during program execution.

continue

Causes execution to jump immediately to the beginning of the loop, skipping any remaining lines after the `continue` statement. For example:

```
while (color != red) {
    incolor /= 2;
    if (incolor >= DARKGRAY)
    continue;
    scrnwrite(bkgndcolor,
        incolor, "*");
}
```

causes the `scrnwrite` statement to be skipped if `incolor` has a value greater than or equal to `DARKGRAY`; the loop is repeated as long as color does not equal `red`.

default

Indicates a statement block to be executed if no match is found for any `case` statement. See `case` and `switch`.

do

Used with `while` to form a loop in which conditions are not checked until the end of the loop. The loop code is executed at least once.

double

A data type signifying floating-point values of double precision.

else

See `if`.

enum

A data type allowing formation of lists of objects, each with a particular integer value.

extern

A storage-class modifier indicating that the variable or function has been declared elsewhere in the program—usually in a separate module. It usually is not used with function declarations in ANSI-compatible compilers because function prototyping can be used instead.

far

A keyword used in microcomputer C compilers as a modifier for pointers and functions. `far` means the pointer uses 32 bits instead of 16, allowing reference to data anywhere within the address space on the 80x86/8 processors. See the section "Memory Models and Memory Management."

float

A type specifier for variables of type `float`.

for

A common statement in C. With a `for` statement, variables can be initialized and incremented within the body of the for loop.

For example:

```
for (i=1; i<= scrnwid; ++i) {
    printf("@");;
    get_another_char();
}
```

In this example, `i=1` is the initializing expression, `i <= scrnwid` is the conditional expression, and `++1` is the loop-counter increment.

fortran

Used by Microsoft C to specify the FORTRAN calling sequence for function parameters. It is similar to the Pascal sequence in order of parameter processing (left to right), and the calling convention is that parameters are passed by reference. Passing by value could be specified if needed.

goto

Causes a jump to a label.

huge

An 80x86/8-specific modifier forcing a pointer variable to use 32 bits. `huge` uses a *normalized* pointer, which means that as much of its value as possible is placed into the segment address portion of the pointer. See the section "Memory Models and Memory Management."

if

A common C statement of the general form:

```
if (condition) {
    block1;
} else {
    block2;
}
```

Braces are not required if the blocks are single statements. The portion starting with else is also optional. The if statement is executed if the condition evaluates to something other than 0 (false). If an else clause is used, block1 is executed if the condition is true (value of 1); otherwise, the else section (block2) is performed.

int

A type specifier for integer variables.

interrupt

A non-ANSI keyword acting as a function modifier signifying a system interrupt routine for use as an interrupt handler.

long

A data type keyword for integers occupying twice the number of bytes occupied by a short integer.

near

An 80x86/8-specific pointer and function modifier specifying the use of 16 bits. See the section "Memory Models and Memory Management."

pascal

A modifier for functions and identifiers signaling the compiler to use Pascal conventions, such as working with function parameters on the stack from left to right, instead of C conventions. See cdecl.

register

A storage modifier specifying that a variable should be stored in a register, if possible.

return

Causes the end of a function and results in a value as specified in the function declaration. For example:

```
char getanswer(void);
{
    char c = 'N';
    c = toupper(getchar());
    if (c == 'Y' || c == 'N')
        return(c);
    else
        return('\0');
}
```

This function returns either the character Y or N, or \0 if the character obtained does not equal Y or N.

---

sizeof

An operator that returns the size of the data object given it as a parameter.

---

signed

A data type modifier in ANSI C for character and integer types; the value may or may not use a plus sign (+) or a minus sign (−).

---

short

A modifier used with integers; `short` is usually the same as `int` on most machines.

---

static

A storage modifier that tells the compiler to retain the variable or function for the duration of the program. The variable retains its previous value between function calls.

---

struct

Used to create complex variables/types ("records" in other languages) composed of "fields" or "members" of various types. See the section "Data Types and Variables" for more information.

switch

A multi-branching statement that more efficiently takes the place of a series of nested if...else statements in C. For example:

```
menuselection =
    toupper(getchar());
switch (menuselection)
{
case 'A' :
    open_file(filename);
    break;
case 'B' :
    read_file(filename);
    parse_input();
    close_file(filename);
    break;
case 'C' :
    write_file(filename);
    close_file(filename);
    break;
case 'Q' :
    quit();
    break;
default :
    error_msg();
}
```

typedef

A keyword that is considered a storage class modifier, but it allows the "creation" (actually the renaming of a preexisting type) of a new variable and function types in C using either simple or complex units. The syntax is

```
typedef <data type> <new name>;
```

For example:

```
typedef int BOOLEAN;
```

Creating a variable using the new type would be

```
BOOLEAN done;
```

which then could take an integer value.

_____

union

A complex data type in C where one variable out of all variables listed in the union is used at any particular time. All variables would start at the same memory location (overlay one another) if they could be used at once. Enough storage is allocated for the largest member, regardless of which is used.

_____

unsigned

A type modifier that signals the compiler to use only positive values and 0 for the data type, such as `int`, `char`, and `long`, but which doubles the effective upper limit of the type. See the section "Data Types and Variables."

_____

void

A new ANSI C keyword that signifies the function does not return anything, denotes an empty parameter list, or makes "generic" pointers compatible with any other type.

_____

volatile

Indicates that the variable can be changed at any time either within the program or even by factors outside the program, such as hardware.

_____

while

A commonly used loop-control keyword. For example:

```
while (!eof(filename)) {
    parse_input();
    make_new_file(outfile);
    close_file();
    quit();
}
```

The loop is executed as long as the condition(s) after the `while` keyword are true. The loop may never be executed if the conditions are false before the loop is first encountered.

_cs, _ds, _es, _ss

These are special modifiers within 8088/86 compilers used with pointers to indicate certain segments should be used. Turbo C permits additional "pseudo-variables" to access all registers (`_AH`, `_AL`, etc.) directly. These rarely are used unless you are doing hardware-related work such as graphics, interrupt routines, and so on.

Functions

The general form for a function declaration is as follows:

```
<return> <name>(<params>)
{
    statements;
    [return();]
}
```

In this syntax, `<return>` is the type of value the function returns, and `<name>` is the name of the function. The `<params>` section is enclosed in parentheses. A parameter is specified by its type and name (the name may be optional). The body of the function consists of one or more statements enclosed within braces. If the `<return>` is not `void`, then the `return` statement must yield a value of the same type as `<return>`.

main()

In a typical C program, there is a special function called `main()`, which is the primary function of the program and which calls all other functions. It is often the first function defined in a program.

Function Prototyping

When function prototypes are used, the parameters are specified within the parameter list when the function is first declared, instead of being written below the function name. The minimum specification is the type of the parameter:

```
void main(int, char *[]);
```

or the actual parameter names can be included:

```
void main(int argc,
    char *argv[]);
```

A function prototype tells the compiler what to look for when it finds the definition of the function or a call to the function. Parameters can be checked for proper type and number whenever the function is called, thereby reducing errors. Prototypes also assist the compiler in knowing whether to use near, far, or huge pointers when compiling under different memory models.

C Standard Library Functions

The ANSI C standard provides for the definitions of numerous routines expected to be in the compiler library. The standard library is divided into 10 main categories: I/O (input/output), string and character, mathematical, time and date, general utilities, character handling, diagnostics, nonlocal jumps, signal handling, and variable argument routines.

Functions related to a category are placed in separate header files. Standard header files as defined by ANSI C are

```
assert.h              setjmp.h
ctype.h               signal.h
errno.h               stdarg.h
float.h               stddef.h
limits.h              stdio.h
locale.h              string.h
math.h                time.h
```

Functions Covered

The functions covered in the following sections are listed in table 11. A function description consists of the following:

❏ Function prototype (function name, parameters, and return value)

❏ A brief description of the function

❏ The "include" file as defined in the ANSI C standard. Compiler differences in the "include" file are noted.

❏ Related functions (families of routines similar in syntax or usage)

"Struck-through" initials after a function indicate that it is not present in the compiler. ~~EC~~ = not in Eco C; ~~TC~~ = not in Turbo C; ~~MSC~~ = not in Microsoft C; ~~LC~~ = not in Lattice C.

Table 11. C Functions Covered in This Section

Diagnostics (assert.h)
```
assert()
```

Character Handling Functions (ctype.h)
```
isalnum()        ispunct()
isalpha()        isspace()
iscntrl()        isupper()
isdigit()        isxdigit()
isgraph()        tolower()
islower()        toupper()
isprint()
```

Standard I/O Functions (stdio.h)
```
clearerr()       fgets()
fclose()         fopen()
feof()           fprint()
ferror()         fputc()
fflush()         fputs()
fgetc()          fread()
fgetpos() (EC)   freopen()
```

fscanf()
fseek()
fsetpos() (EC)
ftell()
fwrite()
getc()
getchar()
gets()
perror()
printf()
putc()
putchar()
puts()
remove() (EC)

rename()
rewind()
scanf()
setbuf()
setvbuf() (EC)
sprintf()
sscanf()
tmpfile() (EC, LC)
tmpnam() (EC)
ungetc()
vfprintf() (LC)
vprintf() (LC)
vsprintf() (LC)

String and Character Handling Functions (string.h)

memchr()
memcmp()
memcpy()
memmove() (LC)
memset()
strcat()
strchr()
strcmp()
strcoll()
strcpy()
strcspn()
strerror() (EC, LC)

strlen()
strncat()
strncmp()
strncpy()
strpbrk()
strrchr()
strspn()
strstr()
strtok()
strxfrm()

Locale-Specific Functions (locale.h) (both not in EC, TC, MSC, LC)

localeconv()

setlocale()

Mathematical Functions (math.h)

acos()
asin()
atan()
atan2()
ceil()
cos()

cosh()
exp()
fabs()
floor()
fmod()
frexp()

```
ldexp()              sin()
log()                sinh()
log10()              sqrt()
modf() (EC)          tan()
pow()                tanh()
```

Time and Date Functions (time.h)

```
asctime()            localtime()
clock()  (TC, LC)    mktime()  (TC, LC)
ctime()              strftime()
difftime() (LC)      time()
gmtime()
```

General Utilities (stdlib.h)

```
abort() (EC)         malloc()
abs()                mblen()
atexit() (EC, LC)    mbstowcs()
atof()               mbtowc()
atoi()               qsort()
atol()               rand()
bsearch() (LC)       realloc()
calloc()             srand()
div() (EC, LC)       strtod() (LC)
exit()               strtol()
free()               strtoul() (EC, LC)
getenv()             system()
labs() (EC)          wcstombs()
ldiv() (EC, LC)      wctomb()
```

Nonlocal Jumps (setjmp.h)

```
longjump()           setjmp()
```

Signal Handling (signal.h)

```
raise()              signal() (ssignal
    (EC, TC, LC)         in TC) (EC)
```

Variable Function Arguments (stdarg.h) (in vargs.h in EC)

```
va_arg()             va_start()
va_end()
```

Compiler Library Comparisons

Current C compilers often differ from the ANSI standard in their library functions. Most microcomputer implementations of C compilers offer system-specific sets of routines, such as `dir.h` for directory routines; `process.h` for creating and terminating new processes; `bios.h` and `dos.h` for BIOS, DOS, and other machine-specific routines; `alloc.h` for memory-handling routines; etc.

In addition, many compilers differ slightly in their arrangement of routine categories, so one routine found in `stdlib.h` in one compiler may be in `alloc.h` in another compiler.

Note: The value `EOF` is used when end-of-file is reached during file operations. The value of `EOF` is normally -1, but it may have other values.

Of the four compilers listed above (EC, TC, MSC, and LC), Microsoft C 5.0 includes the most standard library functions found in the ANSI C Draft Standard. Microsoft C, however, lacks `localeconv()`, `setlocale()`, and others mentioned later. Some of the predefined macros are also missing, and some are different in other aspects.

Turbo C 1.5 lacks `clock()`, `localeconv()`, `mktime()`, `raise()`, and `setlocale()`. `signal()` is named `ssignal()`, and `srand()` is called `randomize()`. Also, Turbo C has the `fgetpos()` and `fsetpos()` functions even though they are not mentioned in the manual.

Lattice C 3.1 does not provide `atexit()`, `bsearch()`, `clock()`, `difftime()`, `div()`, `ldiv()`, `localeconv()`, `memmove()`, `mktime()`, `raise()`, `setlocale()`, `strerror()`, `strtod()`, `strtoul()`, `tmpfile()`, `va_arg()`, `va_end()`, `va_start()`, `vfprintf()`, `vprintf()`, and `vsprintf()` along with other ANSI Draft Standard features.

Ecosoft C does not include `abort()`, `atexit()`, `div()`, `fgetpos()`, `fsetpos()`, `labs()`, `ldiv()`, `localeconv()`, `memmove()`, `modf()`, `raise()`, `remove()`, `setlocale()`, `setvbuf()`, `signal()`, `strerror()`, `strtoul()`, `tmpfile()`, and `tmpnam()`. Ecosoft C does offer the `strftime()` function.

None of the compilers offer any support for the multibyte (special foreign language) characters through the functions `mblen()`, `mbtowc()`, `mbstowcs()`, `strcoll()`, `strxfrm()`, `wctomb()`, or `wcstombs()`.

Diagnostics—assert.h

assert( )

```
void assert(int expression);
```

The `assert()` function tests the conditions represented by `expression` and prints a message of the format.

```
Assertion failed: file
        <filename>, line <linenum>
```

where `file` and `line number` refer to the source file where the call to `assert()` occurred. If `assert()` fails, it will call the function `abort()` to end the program. The normally undefined name `NDEBUG` can be defined to make any calls to `assert()` ineffective.

Include file

`assert.h`

Related functions

`abort()`

Character Handling Functions— ctype.h

A character (char) variable also can be used as a parameter for these functions and is evaluated in the same way as the expected integer parameter.

isalnum( )

```
int isalnum(int c);
```

Checks whether a character is alphanumeric (A-Z, a-z, 0-9).

Include file
ctype.h

Related functions
```
isalpha(), iscntrl(), isdigit(),
isgraph(), islower(), isprint(),
ispunct(), isspace(), isupper(),
isxdigit()
```

Returns
Nonzero value if alphanumeric, otherwise 0

isalpha( )

```
int isalpha(int c);
```

Checks whether a character is a letter of the alphabet (A-Z, a-z).

Include file
ctype.h

Related functions
    isalnum(), iscntrl(), isdigit(),
    isgraph(), islower(), isprint(),
    ispunct(), isspace(), isupper(),
    isxdigit()

Returns
Nonzero value if in alphabet, otherwise 0

iscntrl( )

```
int iscntrl(int c);
```

Checks whether a character is a control character or the delete character (decimal 0 to 31, and 127).

Include file
ctype.h

Related functions
    isalnum(), isalpha(), isdigit(),
    isgraph(), islower(), isprint(),
    ispunct(), isspace(), isupper(),
    isxdigit()

Returns
Nonzero value if control character, otherwise 0

isdigit( )

```
int isdigit(int c);
```

Checks whether a character is a digit (0-9).

Include file
ctype.h

Related functions
```
isalnum(), isalpha(), iscntrl(),
isgraph(), islower(), isprint(),
ispunct(), isspace(), isupper(),
isxdigit()
```

Returns
Nonzero value if a digit, otherwise 0

isgraph( )

```
int isgraph(int c);
```

Checks whether a character is a printable character, excluding the space character (decimal 32).

Include file
```
ctype.h
```

Related functions
```
isalnum(), isalpha(), iscntrl(),
isdigit(), islower(), isprint(),
ispunct(), isspace(), isupper(),
isxdigit()
```

Returns
Nonzero value if printable, otherwise 0

islower( )

```
int islower(int c);
```

Checks whether a character is a lowercase letter (a-z).

Include file
```
ctype.h
```

Related functions
```
isalnum(), isalpha(), iscntrl(),
isdigit(), isgraph(), isprint(),
ispunct(), isspace(), isupper(),
isxdigit()
```

Returns
Nonzero value if lowercase, otherwise 0

isprint( )

```
int isprint(int c);
```

Checks whether a character is printable
(decimal 32-126).

Include file
```
ctype.h
```

Related functions
```
isalnum(), isalpha(), iscntrl(),
isdigit(), isgraph(), islower(),
ispunct(), isspace(), isupper(),
isxdigit()
```

Returns
Nonzero value if printable, otherwise 0

ispunct( )

```
int ispunct(int c);
```

Checks whether a character is a punctuation character,
which in this function means any printable character that
is neither a control character nor an alphanumeric
character (decimal 32-47, 58-63, 91-96, and 123-126).

Include file
ctype.h

Related functions
isalnum(), isalpha(), iscntrl(),
isdigit(), isgraph(), islower(),
isprint(), isspace(), isupper(),
isxdigit()

Returns
Nonzero value if punctuation, otherwise 0

isspace( )

```
int isspace(int c);
```

Checks whether a character is "whitespace" (space,
carriage return, horizontal or vertical tab, new line, or
form feed).

Include file
ctype.h

Related functions
isalnum(), isalpha(), iscntrl(),
isdigit(), isgraph(), islower(),
isprint(), ispunct(), isupper(),
isxdigit()

Returns
Nonzero value is whitespace, otherwise 0

isupper( )

```
int isupper(int c);
```

Checks whether a character is an uppercase character
(A-Z).

Include file
ctype.h

Related functions
isalnum(), isalpha(), iscntrl(),
isdigit(), isgraph(), islower(),
isprint(), ispunct(), isspace(),
isxdigit()

Returns
Nonzero value if uppercase, otherwise 0

isxdigit( )

```
int isxdigit(int c);
```

Checks whether a character is a valid hexadecimal digit
(0-9, A- F, a-f).

Include file
ctype.h

Related functions
isalnum(), isalpha(), iscntrl(),
isdigit(), isgraph(), islower(),
isprint(), ispunct(), isspace(),
isupper()

Returns
Nonzero value if hexadecimal, otherwise 0

tolower( )

```
int tolower(int c);
```

Converts a character into a lowercase character (a-z) if
possible. There is also a macro _tolower().

Include file

ctype.h

Related functions

toupper(), _tolower(), _toupper()

Returns

Character converted to lowercase or unchanged character

toupper( )

```
int toupper(int c);
```

Converts a character into an uppercase character (A-Z) if possible. The macro _toupper() is also available.

Include file

ctype.h

Related functions

tolower(), _tolower, _toupper()

Returns

Character converted to uppercase or unchanged character

Standard I/O Functions—stdio.h

clearerr( )

```
void clearerr(FILE *stream)
```

This function is used to reset error conditions so that the same error is not continuously reported by another function such as ferror(). The end-of-file indicator is also set to 1 by clearerr().

Include files
stdio.h

Related functions
feof(), ferror(),perror(), rewind()

fclose( )

```
int fclose(FILE *stream);
```

Closes the file stream. Normally, all buffers associated with the file are flushed to disk before closing. The buffers are freed to the memory pool unless set by setbuf() or setvbuf(). It is an error to try to close a file that is already closed.

Include file
stdio.h

Related functions
fflush(), fopen(),freopen()

Returns
0 if successful or error as integer value

feof( )

```
int feof(FILE *stream);
```

Checks for end-of-file of the connected stream's file indicator. When end-of-file is reached (by reading "past" the end of the file), feof() continues to return a nonzero value until the file indicator is moved by using fseek(), rewind(), or another similar function or until the stream's error status has been cleared using clearerr(). This is easier to use than checking the value of getc() when working with a file. eof() performs the same type function but on a file handle. feof() is especially useful with binary files.

Include file

stdio.h

Related functions

eof(), ferror(), fseek(), getc(),
putc(), rewind(), clearerr()

Returns

0; but when end-of-file is reached, returns a nonzero
value

ferror( )

    int ferror(FILE *stream);

This function tests the stream to see whether a read or
write error has occurred. ferror() remains set until
clearerr() or rewind() is called to reset it or until
the file is closed as with fclose().

Include file

stdio.h

Related functions

clearerr(), eof(), getc(), perror(),
putc(), rewind(), fclose()

Returns

0; but when error has occurred, returns a nonzero value

fflush( )

    int fflush(FILE *stream);

Writes the contents of the stream's output buffer to a file
and clears the buffer's contents. The stream remains
open. It is not widely used, because terminating a
program or closing a file typically flushes the buffers. A

recent change to the ANSI draft standard states that using `fflush(NULL)` would be the same as flushing all buffers of any files open.

Include file
stdio.h

Related functions
fopen(), freopen(), fclose(), fread(), fwrite()

Returns
0; but when write error occurs, returns a nonzero value

fgetc( )

```
int fgetc(FILE *stream);
```

This function reads the next character from the stream. Use feof() to determine if end-of-file has been.

Include file
stdio.h

Related functions
feof(), fread(), getc(), getchar()

Returns
Character as integer value, or EOF if end-of-file is reached

fgets( )

```
char *fgets(char *s, int n,
     FILE *stream);
```

fgets() reads characters from the stream until it has gotten n-1 characters, then stores them in the string pointed to by *s. fgets() continues until it detects a newline, reaches EOF, or reaches the n-1 limit.

If a newline is detected, it is kept as part of the string. If a null pointer is returned, use feof() or ferror() to tell what the error is.

Include file
stdio.h

Related functions
feof(), ferror(),gets()

Returns
Pointer to string, or NULL in case of error.

fgetpos( )

```
int fgetpos(FILE *stream,
     fpos_t *pos);
```
(EC and LC; not mentioned in TC manual but included)

The function fgetpos() stores the position of the file indicator from stream in *pos. fsetpos() then can be used to set the file indicator position. fgetpos() was designed to work with files larger than what could be handled by fseek() and ftell().

Include file
stdio.h

Related functions
fseek(), fsetpos(),ftell()

Returns
Positions (*pos) or nonzero value if not successful

fopen( )

```
FILE *fopen(const char *filename,
const char *mode);
```

The function `fopen()` opens the file `filename` using the mode provided and associates the file with a stream.

Include file
stdio.h

Related functions
`fclose()`, `fflush()`, `freopen()`

Returns
Pointer to stream, or null pointer if unsuccessful

If no `filename` as given exists, a new file is created; otherwise, the file's contents are erased unless the append mode is used.

fprint( )

```
int fprintf(FILE *stream, const char
*format, ...);
```

See the special section on the `printf()` family later in this section.

Include file
stdio.h

Related functions
`printf()`, `sprintf()`, `vprintf()`, `putc()`, `puts()`

Returns
Number of characters written, or a negative value (EOF) when an error occurs

fputc( )

```
int fputc(int c, FILE *stream);
```

The function fputc() writes a character to a file pointed to by stream. fputc() basically operates just like putc(). putchar() writes the character to the device stdout.

Include file
stdio.h

Related functions
putc(), putchar(), puts(), fputs(), fgets()

Returns
Character just written or EOF when an error occurs

fputs( )

```
int fputs(const char *s,
     FILE *stream);
```

Writes to a file an entire string pointed to by *s. The similar function puts() writes the string to stdout.

Include file
stdio.h

Related functions
puts(), putc(), gets(), fgets()

Returns
Nonzero value or EOF when an error occurs

fread( )

```
size_t fread(void *ptr, size_t
     size, size_t nmemb,
     FILE *stream);
```

fread() reads from a file nmemb elements, each of
which are of size size, and stores them in the buffer
pointed to by *ptr. size_t is an unsigned integer
defined in the header file stddef.h.

Include file
stdio.h

Related functions
fwrite(), fscanf(), getc(), gets()

Returns
Number of elements successfully read or 0 when an
error occurs

freopen( )

```
FILE *freopen(const char *filename,
     const char *mode, FILE *stream);
```

The function freopen() replaces stream with
filename using mode (r, w, a, rb+, etc.). The stream
is closed whether or not it was open.

Include file
stdio.h

Related functions
fclose(), fflush(), fopen()

Returns
Pointer to stream if successful, or a null pointer when
an error occurs

fscanf( )

```
int fscanf(FILE *stream, const
     char *format, ...);
```

This function allows formatted input from the file via input fields and converts the input to the specified format. See the special section on the scanf() family in this section for more information.

Include file

stdio.h

Related functions

scanf(), sscanf(), vscanf()

Returns

Number of characters input (including 0), or EOF on error

fseek( )

```
int fseek(FILE *stream, long int
     offset, int whence);
```

The function fseek() positions the file indicator of stream by telling it a starting point (whence) within the file and the distance in bytes (offset) to go from that point, thus allowing random access. The function ftell() can be used to calculate offset. ANSI specifies whence as three constants:

```
SEEK_SET = 0 = beginning of the file;
SEEK_CUR = 1 = current position; and
SEEK_END = 2 = end of the file.
```

In order to work with files larger than 64K, offset should be cast to a long integer. fseek() may have problems calculating the correct position within text files unless offset is set to 0L or ftell() is used along with SEEK_SET. fseek(), therefore, usually is

used on binary files. It also clears any prior calls to
ungetc() or end-of-file.

Include file
stdio.h

Related functions
fgetpos(), fsetpos(), ftell()

Returns
0, or nonzero value if unsuccessful

fsetpos( )

```
int fsetpos(FILE *stream,
      const fpos_t *pos);
```
(EC and LC only; not mentioned in TC manual)

This function positions the file indicator of stream at
the position pointed to by *pos, which has been
calculated by fgetpos().

Include file
stdio.h

Related functions
errno(), fgetpos(), fseek(), ftell()

Returns
0, or a nonzero value upon error

ftell( )

```
long int ftell(FILE *stream);
```

The function ftell() reports the current position of
the file indicator of stream—from the beginning of the
file in most cases. If an error occurs, errno() should
be used to check what actually happened.

Include file
      stdio.h

Related functions
      errno(), fgetpos(), fseek(), fsetpos()

Returns
      Position from the beginning of file as a long int; -1 on
      error

fwrite( )

```
size_t fwrite(const void *ptr, size_t
      size, size_t nmemb,
      FILE *stream);
```

This function writes nmemb, each with a size of size
to the stream beginning at the position pointed to by
*ptr.

Include file
      stdio.h

Related functions
      fopen(), fread(), getc(), gets(), putc(),
      puts()

Returns
      Number of items actually written, or a short count upon
      error (< nmemb)

getc( )

```
int getc(FILE *stream);
```

getc() reads a character from stream and readies
the file indicator for the next character. Use feof() to

test the end-of-file condition. getc() is a macro and is otherwise the same as fgetc(). ungetc() can push a character back onto the file to be read again by getc().

Include file

stdio.h

Related functions

```
ungetc(), feof(), fgetc(), fgetchar(),
fgets(), getchar(), gets(), putc(),
puts(), ungetc()
```

Returns

Integer value of character read, or EOF if end-of-file is reached

getchar( )

```
int getchar(void);
```

The function getchar() gets the next character from stdin and sets the file indicator to read the next character.

Include file

stdio.h

Related functions

```
ungetc(), feof(), fgetc(), fgetchar(),
fgets(), getc(), gets(), putc(), puts(),
ungetc()
```

Returns

Integer value of next character, or EOF

gets( )

```
char *gets(char *s);
```

The function gets() gets a null-terminated (normal C) string from the device stdin and continues reading characters until a newline or EOF is reached. The newline is not added to the end of the string.

Include file
stdio.h

Related functions
feof(), fgetc(), fgetc(), fgetchar(),
fgets(), getc(), putc(), puts(),
ungetc()

Returns
Pointer to string just read, or null pointer if an error occurs

perror( )

```
void perror(const char *s);
```

The function perror() prints the string *s on stderr (standard error output device) along with a colon and a space followed by a brief message corresponding to errno, and then a newline.

Include file
stdio.h

Related functions
errno (actually an integer value), ferror(),
strerror()

printf( )

```
int printf(const char *format, ...);
```

See the special section on the `printf()` family later in this section.

Include file
stdio.h

Related functions
fprintf(), sprintf(), vprintf()

Returns
Number of characters output, or 0 if an error occurs

putc( )

```
int putc(int c, FILE *stream);
```

The function `putc()` writes a character to `stream`. Error conditions should be checked with `feof()` to see whether that condition actually exists. It is implemented as a macro and functions like `fputc()`.

Include file
stdio.h

Related functions
feof(), fgetc(), fgetchar(), fgets(), getc(), gets(), putchar(), puts(), ungetc()

Returns
Character as integer value, or EOF if an error occurs

putchar( )

```
int putchar(int c);
```

The function `putchar()` writes a character to the device `stdout`. Error conditions are checked with `feof()`. `putchar()` is also implemented as a macro.

Include file
stdio.h

Related functions
feof(), fgetc(), fgetchar(), fgets(), getc(), gets(), puts(), ungetc()

Returns
Character as integer value, or EOF if an error occurs

puts( )

```
int puts(const char *s);
```

The function `puts()` writes a string to the `stdout` device and adds a newline, even if a newline already exists.

Include file
stdio.h

Related functions
fgetc(), getc(), fgetchar(), gets(), fgets(), ungetc(), putchar(), printf()

Returns
0, or nonzero (EOF, non-ANSI) value if an error occurs

remove( )

```
int remove(const char *filename); (EC)
```

This function deletes the file `filename`. The effects if the file is open are compiler-specific; but once "removed," the file should no longer be accessible.

Include file
stdio.h

Related functions
rename()

Returns
0, or nonzero value when an error occurs

rename( )

```
int rename(const char *old,
     const char *new);
```

Changes the name of file called `old` to `new`. On the PC, the compiler may allow a different directory in `new` from that in `old` and thereby move the file from one directory to another (the drive, if given, must be the same). If the file name given by `new` already exists or is open, the actions are compiler-specific.

Include file
stdio.h

Related functions
remove()

Returns
0, or nonzero value if not successful

rewind( )

```
void rewind(FILE *stream);
```

rewind() moves the file indicator to the beginning of the file stream and clears any existing error conditions.

Include file
stdio.h

Related functions
fseek(), fsetpos()

scanf( )

```
int scanf(const char *format, ...);
```

See the special section on the scanf() family later in this section.

Include file
stdio.h

Related functions
fscanf(), sscanf(), vscanf()

Returns
Number of characters input (including 0) or EOF on error

setbuf( )

```
void setbuf(FILE *stream, char *buf);
```

The function setbuf() allows the programmer to specify a buffer for stream. The buffer is pointed to by *buf and must be BUFSIZE (defined in stdio.h also) in size. The buffer may be NULL, in which case buffering is effectively turned off. The variable buf should be static or global in scope unless you close the file within the block in which buf is declared.

Include file
stdio.h

Related functions
fclose(), fopen(), setvbuf()

setvbuf( )

```
int setvbuf(FILE *stream, char *buf
        int mode, size_t size); (EC)
```

Establishes a buffer for stream pointed to by *buf with a size that should be BUFSIZE as defined in stdio.h. No buffering occurs if buf is NULL. The third parameter, mode, corresponds to one of three integer constants:

1. _IOFBF = fully buffered

2. _IOLBF = line buffered, or the buffer is flushed after every line, or the buffer is flushed when a newline is detected

3. _IONBF = no buffering.

Include file
stdio.h

Related functions
fclose(), fopen(), setbuf()

Returns
0 if successful or nonzero value if problems occur

sprintf( )

```
int sprintf(char *s, const
    char *format, ...);
```

See the special section on the scanf() family later in this section.

Include file
stdio.h

Related functions
fprintf(), vprintf()

Returns
Number of characters output, or 0 if an error occurs

sscanf( )

```
int sscanf(const char *s, const
    char *format, ...);
```

See the special section on the scanf() family later in this section.

Include file
stdio.h

Related functions
scanf(), fscanf(), vscanf()

Returns
Number of characters input (including 0), or EOF on error

tmpfile( )

FILE *tmpfile(void); (E̶C̶ and L̶C̶)

Creates and opens a temporary file in the wb+ mode, which will be closed and removed when the program ends.

Include file

stdio.h

Related functions

fopen(), tmpnam()

Returns

Pointer to stream just created, or null pointer on error

tmpnam( )

char *tmpnam(char *s); (~~EC~~)

tmpnam() creates a unique file name up to TMP_MAX (in stdio.h) times, which must be at least 25 times. The names will not conflict with any other names and are meant to be temporary. tmpnam() creates storage for the name even if *s() is NULL.

Include file

stdio.h

Related functions

tmpfile()

Returns

Character pointer to new name *s, or NULL pointer on failure

ungetc( )

int ungetc(int c, FILE *stream);

This function puts a character (except EOF) back onto stream to be read again by either fgetc(), getc(), or `getchar()` if file buffering is on, and at least one character already has been read. Calls to `fopen()` or `freopen()` void any characters in storage to be put back. This also means the file indicator is moved back one position for each character, so functions changing the indicator's position (for example, `fseek()`, `fsetpos()`) affect `ungetc()`'s memory also.

Include file
stdio.h

Related functions
fgetc(), fgetchar(), fgets(), fopen(),
getc(), gets(), freopen(), getchar,
fseek(), putchar(), puts()

Returns
Integer value of the character, or EOF on error

vfprintf( )

```
int vfprintf(FILE *stream, const
    char*format, va_list arg); (LC)
```

See the special section on the `printf()` family later in this section.

Include file
stdio.h

Related functions
fprintf(), printf(), vprintf(),
vsprintf()

Returns
Number of characters output, or 0 if error

vprintf( )

```
int vprintf(const char
     *format, va_list arg); (LC)
```

See the special section on the `printf()` family later in this section.

Include file
stdio.h

Related functions
```
fprintf(), printf(), vfprintf(),
vsprintf()
```

Returns
Number of characters output, or 0 if error

vsprintf( )

```
int vsprintf(char *s, const
     char *format, va_list arg); (LC)
```

See the special section on the `printf()` family later in this section.

Include file
stdio.h

Related functions
```
fprintf(), printf(), vfprintf(),
vprintf()
```

Returns
Number of characters output, or 0 if error

C Quick Reference ========================

The printf( ) Family

```
int fprintf(FILE *stream, const char
      *format, ...);
int printf(const char *format, ...);
int sprintf(char *s, const char
      *format,...);
int vfprintf(FILE *stream, const char
      *format, va_list arg);
int vprintf(const char *format,
      va_list arg);
int vsprintf(char *s, const char
      *format, va_list arg);
```

Note: The functions vfprintf(), vprintf(), and
vsprintf() are not in LC.

These functions accept input formatted according to
certain specifications and send it to different places:
files, standard system devices, strings, etc. Some
compilers also have other printf functions, such as
cprintf(), that are not part of the ANSI Draft
Standard and send output only to the console (screen).

fprintf() should have a valid stream (file) as the
first parameter in order to direct output to the stream;
this can include also the standard system devices of
stdout and stderr. sprintf() causes formatted
output to be placed in a string given as the first
parameter.

The general form of the format specification string is:

```
"%[flags][width][.precision]
      [F, N, h or l]type"
```

Type Characters

Table 12 shows the format specifications that tell the
compiler which type is expected from the argument list.
If the argument does not match the format type, output
may not be correct.

Table 12. Type Characters

Format Specifier	Explanation
Integers	
d, i	Signed decimal integers and longs
o	Signed octal integer
u	Unsigned decimal integers and longs
x, X	Unsigned hexidecimal conversion
Floats	
f	Signed floating point value
e, E	Signed floating point value with exponential notation
g, G	Signed float of either e or f format
Characters	
c	Single character
s	String
%	(actually %%) prints percent sign
Pointers	
n	Number of characters output so far
p	Prints address

The flag characters specify output characteristics (see table 13). Right-justification is the default.

Table 13. Flag Characters

Format Specifier	Explanation
−	Causes left-justification, padding with blanks
0	Zeros are used to pad instead of spaces if a field length is given.
+	Output always begins with + or −.
blank	Positive values begin with a blank.
#	An alternate number form is used in the conversion of e, E, f, g, G, o, x, and X formats.

Table 14 shows the characters denoting the width of the field in which output is printed.

Table 14. Field Width Specifications

Specifier	Example	Explanation
n	%10s	A minimum of n characters are printed.
		Note: Strings are not necessarily affected by the width specification; it is the *precision* portion which causes a different length string to be output. Example: %.4s causes reference to be output as refe, but %4s causes the entire string to be output as reference.
*	%*f	The width specifier is supplied by the argument list.

The width specifier must appear *before* the argument to be formatted. This allows the width and precision to be supplied at runtime. Example: %*.*f would require arguments of 5, 3, and 82.1493 and would effectively use a format of %5.3f to cause 82.149 as output.

Table 15. Format Precision Specifications

Specifier	Explanation
none or .0	Default precision is used: d, i, o, u, x, X = 1; e, E, f = 6, no decimal with .0; g, G = all digits; s = all characters; c = nothing;
.n	n positions are used as output.
*	The precision is given in the argument list (see table 13).

Table 16. Input Size Specification

Specifier	Explanation
F	The argument is considered to be a `far` pointer (not ANSI C).
N	The argument is considered to be a `near` pointer (not ANSI C).
h	The argument must be of type `short int`.
l	The argument must be of type `long int`.
L (ANSI C)	The argument is of type `long double` and can be used with e, E, f, g, or G.

Include file

stdio.h

Returns

Most return the number of characters actually output, or a negative value if an error occurs. For those functions sending output to a string, the terminating null character is not counted in the number of characters output.

The scanf( ) Family

```
int fscanf(FILE *stream, const
     char *format, ...);
int scanf(const char *format, ...);
int sscanf(const char *s, const
     char *format, ...);
```

Description

This family of functions allows input of values from the keyboard, from a string, or from a file. The format specifications are similar to those used by `printf()`, so only the differences are pointed out here. The function stops reading input when one of the following conditions is met:

1. The next character is EOF.

2. The end of the format string has been reached.

3. A mismatch has occurred between the format string and the input fields or between the control character set and the character input.

Format Specification

The general form of the format specification string is

```
"%[*][width][F or N][h or l]type"
```

Example:

```
"%4s"
```

All lowercase type characters as from scanf() are allowed in ANSI C (%d, %i, %o, %u, %x, %c, %s, %e, %f, %g, and %%). Many microcomputer implementations allow the uppercase counterparts also (same as for printf()).

Note: If %s is used, the string to hold input must be large enough for all characters *and* a terminating null character, which is automatically appended.

Brackets ([]) may also be included and are placed in one argument, which is of type char *. The brackets contain a set of characters allowed during input. This makes the brackets useful for "field checks," such as allowing only the digits 0-9 ([0123456789]) when inputting unsigned integers.

If the circumflex (^), called also the "top hat" or "caret," immediately follows the opening bracket, it signals to the compiler to allow negation of input. Any other position in the set has no special meaning.

The right and left brackets may be included if they are immediately at the beginning of the set. This facility is useful for fields not containing whitespace.

The asterisk (*) can function here in assignment suppression. The input field is scanned but not used to fill the next argument in the function parameter list.

Field width may be specified by using an integer value between the % sign and the type—for example, %9f. No precision can be specified.

The same modifiers are allowed as for printf(): F, N, h, l, or L.

scanf() functions normally stop reading input to a particular field if the width is exceeded, the character does not match what is in the control set, a whitespace character is detected, or there is a format string conflict.

Include file
```
#include <stdio.h>
```

Returns
The number of fields successfully processed are returned by these functions, and a negative value (-1 = EOF) is returned if the end-of-file is discovered during input.

String and Character Functions— string.h

memchr( )

```
void *memchr(const void *s, int c,
size_t n);
```

Scans the object pointed to by *s for the character c within the first n characters of the object.

Include file
```
string.h
```

Related functions
    strchr(), strstr()

Returns
    Pointer to the located character, or a NULL pointer if it
    is not in the object pointed to by s

memcmp( )

```
int memcmp(const unsigned char *s1,
     const unsigned char *s2,
     size_t n);
```

memcmp() compares two strings, s1 and s2, for n
number of characters to see whether they differ.

Include file
    string.h

Related functions
    strcmp

Returns
    0 if s1=s2, an integer > 0 if s1 > s2, or an integer < 0
    if s1 < s2

memcpy( )

```
void *memcpy(void *s1, const
     void *s2, size_t n);
```

Copies n characters from the memory location pointed
to by s2 to the location pointed to by s1.

Include file
    string.h

Related functions
    memmove(), strcpy(), strncpy()

Returns

void ("generic") pointer to s1

memmove( )

```
void *memmove(void *s1, const
    void *s2, sizt_t n); (EC and LC)
```

memmove() moves n characters from the region
pointed to by s2 and putting the characters into the
region pointed to by s1. memmove() works correctly
even if s1 and s2 overlap.

Include file

string.h

Related functions

memcpy(), strcpy(), strncpy

Returns

void pointer pointing to s1

memset( )

```
void *memset(void *s, int c,
    size_t n);
```

Sets n characters at s to the value c.

Include file

string.h

Related functions

calloc(), strcpy(), strncpy(), memcpy()

Returns

Pointer to the object s

strcat( )

```
char *strcat(char *s1, const
     char *s2);
```

Appends the string s2 to the end of string s1, over-writing anything in memory after s1. The null termina-tor of s1 is replaced by the first character of s2.

Include file
string.h

Related functions
strncat(), strchr(), strcpy(),
strncpy()

Returns
Pointer to string s1

strchr( )

```
char *strchr(const char *s, int c);
```

Searches the string s for character c.

Include file
string.h

Related functions
memchr(), strstr(), strrstr()

Returns
Character pointer to c within the string s, or a null pointer if not found

strcmp( )

```
int strcmp(const unsigned char
    *s1, const unsigned char *s2);
```

Compares n characters of s1 to s2.

Include file
string.h

Related functions
memcmp

Returns
0 if s1=s2, an integer > 0 if s1 > s2, or an integer < 0
if s1 < s2

strcoll( )

```
int strcoll(const char *s1, const
    char *s2);
```
(ANSI only, not in EC, TC, MSC, or LC)

Compares two strings according to the locale of the
program. Special characters of a foreign language
(accents, diacritical marks, and so on) are also taken
into consideration.

Include file
string.h

Related functions
strcmp(), strncmp(), strxfrm()

Returns
0 if s1=s2, an integer > 0 if s1 > s2, or an integer < 0
if s1 < s2

strcpy( )

```
char *strcpy(char *s1, const
      char *s2);
```

Copies the contents of string s2 into string s1. If the two strings overlap, the results are unpredictable. The copying takes place even if they are of different lengths, and the terminating null character is included.

Include file
string.h

Related functions
strncpy(), memcpy(), memmove()

Returns
Character pointer to s1

strcspn( )

```
size_t strcspn(const char *s1,
      const char *s2);
```

Returns the number of characters at the beginning of s1 that are not in s2.

Include file
string.h

Related functions
strspn(), strchr(), strstr(), strpbrk()

Returns
Number of characters at the beginning of string s1 not in s2, or 0 if the first letter of s1 is in s2

strerror( )

```
char *strerror(int errnum); (EC and LC)
```

Returns an error message corresponding to the errnum
(error number) given as a parameter.

Include file
string.h

Related functions
ferror(), perror()

Returns
Pointer to an error-message string

strlen( )

```
size_t strlen(const char *s);
```

Returns the length of the string at s, not counting the
null terminator.

Include file
string.h

Related functions
strcmp(), strncmp()

Returns
Size of the string

strncat( )

```
char *strncat(char *s1, const
      char *s2, size_t n);
```

Concatenates n characters from s2 to s1. If n is larger
than length of s2, process ends with the null terminator.

C Quick Reference

Include file
    string.h

Related functions
    strcat(), strchr(), strcpy(), strncpy()

Returns
    Character pointer to string s1

---

strncmp( )

```
int strncmp(const unsigned char *s1,
      const unsigned char *s2,
      size_t n);
```

Compares n characters in s1 and s2.

Include file
    string.h

Related functions
    strcmp(), memcmp()

Returns
    0 if s1=s2, an integer > 0 if s1 > s2, or an integer < 0
    if s1 < s2

---

strncpy( )

```
char strncpy(char *s1, const
      char *s2, size_t n);
```

Copies n characters from s2 to s1. If s2 has fewer than
n characters, s1 is padded with spaces.

Include file
    string.h

Related functions
    strcpy(), memcpy(), memmove()

Returns
    Character pointer to s1

strpbrk( )

```
char *strpbrk(const char *s1,
        const char *s2);
```

Searches string s1 for the first occurrence of any
character found in the string pointed to by s2.

Include file
    string.h

Related functions
    strspn(), strcspn(), strchr(), strstr()

Returns
    Character pointer to the first character of s2 that
    is in s1

strrchr( )

```
char *strrchr(const char *s, int c);
```

Searches string s for the *last* occurrence of character c.

Include file
    string.h

Related functions
    strchr(), strstr(), strspn(), strcspn()

Returns
    Pointer to character if found or NULL pointer otherwise

strspn( )

```
size_t strspn(const char *s1,
    const char *s2);
```

Calculates the number of characters at the beginning of s1 that are all found in the string s2.

Include file
string.h

Related functions
strchr(), strstr(), strcspn(), strrchr

Returns
Number of characters at the beginning of string s1 that are in s2, or 0 if none of s2 is found in s1

strstr( )

```
char *strstr(const char *s1,
    const char *s2);
```

The function strstr() searches the string s1 for the substring of s2 (the entire string, not just individual characters), so it too acts as a "parser."

Include file
string.h

Related functions
strchr(), strrchr(), strspn(), strcspn()

Returns
Pointer to the beginning of s1 where the characters are found, or a null pointer if not found

strtok( )

```
char *strtok(char *s1, const
      char *s2);
```

Parses the string at s1 into tokens delimited by the
characters at s2.

Include file
string.h

Related functions
```
strchr(), strrchr(), strspn(),
strcspn(), strstr()
```

Returns
Pointer to the token, or a null pointer if there is no
token

strxfrm( )

```
size_t strxfrm(char *s1, const
      char *s2, size_t n);
```
(ANSI only, not in EC, TC, MSC, or LC)

This function changes the string s2 and puts the result
into s1, working on n number of characters during the
change. It takes locale-specific information (that is,
foreign languages, nationalities, and so on) into account
during the transformation.

Include file
string.h

Related functions
strcmp(), strcoll(), strncmp()

Returns
Length of the transformed string at s1

Locale-specific Functions— locale.h

These functions use the `lconv` structure, which contains information regarding number formats, currency symbols, etc., for various nationalities. The members of `lconv` are as follows:

`char *decimal_point;`
  decimal point for nonmonetary values

`char *thousands_sep;`
  thousands separator for nonmonetary values */

`char *grouping;`
  string showing the size of groups of digits in nonmonetary values

`char *int_curr_symbol;`
  international currency symbol of up to four characters

`char *currency_symbol;`
  local currency symbol

`char *mon_decimal_point;`
  decimal point for monetary values

`char *mon_thousands_sep;`
  separator for thousands in monetary values

`char *mon_grouping;`
  string showing the size of groups of digits in monetary values

`char *positive_sign;`
  symbol for positive sign

`char *negative_sign;`
  symbol for negative sign

`char frac_digits;`
  number of digits displayed to the right of the decimal position in monetary quantities

`char p_cs_precedes;`
  1 if the currency symbol precedes the monetary value, 0 if after it

```
char p_sep_by_space;
```
1 if the currency symbol is separated by a space from the monetary value, 0 if not

```
char n_cs_precedes;
```
1 if the currency symbol precedes the negative monetary value, 0 if not

```
char n_sep_by_space;
```
1 if the currency symbol is separated by a space from a negative monetary value, 0 if not

```
char p_sign_posn;
```
indicates the position of the positive sign for a monetary value

```
char n_sign_posn;
```
indicates the position of the negative sign for a monetary value

p_sign_posn and n_sign_posn may have the following values:

❏ 0 = parentheses around the quantity

❏ 1 = sign string precedes the quantity

❏ 2 = sign string succeeds the quantity

❏ 3 = sign string immediately precedes the currency symbol

❏ 4 = sign string immediately succeeds the currency symbol

localeconv( )

```
struct lconv *localeconv(void);
```
(ANSI only, not in EC, TC, MSC, or LC)

This function supplies information for filling in the locale structure for numeric values. When the structure is set, it may not be changed by the program unless further calls to localeconv() or setlocale() are made.

Include file

```
locale.h
```

Related functions

```
setlocale
```

Returns

Pointer to the structure filled in with the appropriate values from the locale information

setlocale( )

```
char *setlocale(int category,
      const char *locale);
```
(ANSI only, not in EC, TC, MSC, or LC)

The `locale` parameter can take the values "C" for the minimum requirements for the C language, and an empty string ("") allows use of the compiler-specific environment. Other compiler-specific values are allowed. The function is used to find out parts or the entire package of information for the locale.

The first parameter `category` can be specified by the following six macros found in `locale.h`:

1. LC_ALL – program's entire locale
2. LC_COLLATE – settings for the `strcoll()` and `strxfrm()` functions
3. LC_CTYPE – sets actions of character handling functions
4. LC_MONETARY – refers to monetary values
5. LC_NUMERIC – refers to non-monetary numeric values
6. LC_TIME – affects the `strftime()` function

Include file

```
locale.h
```

Related functions

```
localeconv(), strcoll(), strxfrm(),
strftime()
```

Returns

String to the category for the new locale, or a null pointer if it cannot be applied

Mathematical Functions—math.h

acos( )

```
double acos(double x);
```

Calculates the arc cosine of x, which must be in the range of -1 to 1. The result is in radians.

Include file

```
math.h
```

Related functions

```
cos(), cosh(), asin(), atan()
```

Returns

Double-precision value for x

asin( )

```
double asin(double x);
```

Calculates the arc sine of x, which must be in the range of -1 to 1. The result is in radians.

Include file

```
math.h
```

Related functions
```
sin(), sinh(), acos(), atan()
```

Returns
Double-precision values occur if x is negative

atan( )

```
double atan(double x);
```

Calculates the arc tangent of x, which must be in the range of -1 to 1, and returns the result in radians.

Include file
```
math.h
```

Related functions
```
tan(), tanh(), acos(), asin()
```

Returns
Double-precision value for x

atan2( )

```
double atan2(double y, double x);
```

The function atan2() calculates the arc tangent of y and x of the value y/x and returns the result in radians.

Include file
```
math.h
```

Related functions
```
tan(), tanh(), atan(), acos(), asin
```

Returns
Double-precision value for y/x

ceil( )

```
double ceil(double x);
```

Returns the smallest integer (as a double) that is greater than x.

Include file
math.h

Related functions
floor(), fmod()

Returns
Double-precision value

cos( )

```
double cos(double x);
```

Calculates the cosine of x which is expressed in radians.

Include file
math.h

Related functions
cosh(), acos()

Returns
Double-precision value of x

cosh( )

```
double cosh(double x);
```

The function cosh() calculates the hyperbolic cosine value of x which is expressed in radians.

Include file
math.h

Related functions
cos(), acos()

Returns
Double-precision value of x

exp( )

```
double exp(double x);
```

Calculates e raised to the xth power.

Include file
math.h

Related functions
log()

Returns
Double-precision value of x

fabs( )

```
double fabs(double x);
```

Returns the absolute value of x.

Include file
math.h

Related functions
abs()

Returns
Double-precision value of x

floor( )

```
double floor(double x);
```

Returns the smallest integer value less than x.

Include file
math.h

Related functions
ceil(), fmod()

Returns
Double-precision value of x

fmod( )

```
double fmod(double x, double y);
```

Returns x modulo y

Include file
math.h

Related functions
ceil(), floor()

Returns
Double-precision value of x/y

frexp( )

```
double frexp(double value, int *exp);
```

This function calculates the mantissa of value so that it is in the range of 0.5 to 1. The function also calculates an integer so that the mantissa times 2 raised to the power of exp equals value (value = mantissa * 2^exp).

Include file
> math.h

Related functions
> ldexp(), modf()

Returns
> Double-precision value of the mantissa

ldexp( )

```
double ldexp(double x, int exp);
```

Returns x after calculating x *2^exp.

Include file
> math.h

Related functions
> frexp(), modf()

Returns
> Double-precision value of x as calculated

log( )

```
double log(double x);
```

Returns the natural log of x, which must be positive.

Include file
> math.h

Related functions
> exp(), log()

Returns
> Double-precision value

log10( )

```
double log10(double x);
```

Computes the base 10 log of x; an error may occur if x is negative.

Include file

math.h

Related functions

log(), exp()

Returns

Double-precision base 10 logarithm of x

modf( )

```
double modf(double value,
        double *iptr); (EC)
```

Returns the fractional portion of value and places the integer portion of value into iptr.

Include file

math.h

Related functions

frexp(), ldexp()

Returns

Fractional portion of value

pow( )

```
double pow(double x, double y);
```

Returns x raised to the power of y. If either x or y is 0, the result is 0. If either is negative, an error may occur.

Include file
    math.h

Related functions
    sqrt()

Returns
    Double-precision value of x to the y

sin( )

```
double sin(double x);
```

Calculates the sine of x which must be in radians.

Include file
    math.h

Related functions
    sinh(), cosin(), cosinh()

Returns
    Double-precision sine of x

sinh( )

```
double sinh(double x);
```

Returns the hyperbolic sine of x which must be in radians.

Include file
    math.h

Related functions
    sin(), cosin(), cosinh()

Returns
> Double-precision hyperbolic sine of x

sqrt( )

```
double sqrt(double x);
```

Returns the square root of x.

Include file
> math.h

Related functions
> pow()

Returns
> Double-precision square root of x

tan( )

```
double tan(double x);
```

Returns the tangent of x which is expressed in radians.

Include file
> math.h

Related functions
> tanh(), atan(), atanh()

Returns
> Double-precision tangent of x

tanh( )

```
double tanh(double x);
```

Returns the hyperbolic tangent of x which is expressed in radians.

Include file
math.h

Related functions
tan(), atan(), atanh()

Returns
Double-precision hyperbolic tangent of x

Time and Date Functions—time.h

struct tm is a data structure that holds time information. The following is a listing of the members of struct tm.

int tm_sec;
 seconds, 0-60. This is to account for a "leap second," which is sometimes added at the end of a calendar quarter.

int tm_min;
 minutes

int tm_hour;
 hours, 0-23

int tm_day;
 day of the month, 1-31

int tm_mon;
 month

int tm_year;
 year from 1900

```
int tm_wday;
    weekday (Sunday=0)
```

```
int tm_yday;
    day of the year, 0-365
```

```
int tm_isdst;
    daylight saving time flag
```

All value ranges except the day of the month start with 0. The daylight saving time flag has three values: *positive* if in effect, *0* if not in effect, or *negative* if information not available.

asctime( )

```
char *asctime(const struct
    tm *timeptr);
```

This function changes the time into a string of the following form:

```
Tue Feb 25 11:21:35 1988\n\0
```

The string should be placed elsewhere or printed before making another call to the function.

Include file
time.h

Related functions
ctime(), time()

Returns
Pointer to the time represented as a string

clock( )

```
clock_t clock(void); (TC, LC)
```

This function determines the processor time used since the start of the program, if possible.

Include file

time.h

Related functions

asctime(), CLK_TCK(), ctime(), macro(),
time()

Returns

Processor time used, which can be changed to seconds
by dividing the value by the macro CLK_TCK; or -1 cast
to the type clock_t if the time is not available

ctime( )

```
char *ctime(const time_t *timer);
```

Creates the same 26-character string as asctime()
but can take the time value from the routine time
directly.

Include file

time.h

Related functions

time(), asctime()

Returns

Character pointer to time represented as a string

difftime( )

```
double difftime(time_t time1,
     time_t time0); (LC)
```

Calculates the difference between time1 and time0
and reports it in seconds.

Include file
    time.h

Related functions
    time(), gmtime(), localtime(),
    asctime()

Returns
    Time in seconds

gmtime( )

```
struct tm *gmtime(const
    time_t *timer);
```

Converts the time into Greenwich Mean Time.

Include file
    time.h

Related functions
    localtime(), ctime(), asctime(), time()

Returns
    Pointer to data structure holding time information, or
    null pointer on error

localtime( )

```
struct tm *localtime(const
    time_t *timer);
```

Converts time information into local time, which may
include converting according to daylight saving time or
the local time zone.

Include file
    time.h

Related functions
gmtime( ), ctime( ), asctime( ), time( )

Returns
Pointer to data structure holding time information, or null pointer on error

mktime( )

```
time_t mktime(struct tm *timeptr);
```
(TC and LC)

Changes the information in the structure pointed to by timeptr into calendar time. The day of the week (tm_wday) and day of the year (tm_yday) values are ignored during conversion, and the ranges may be different.

Include file
time.h

Related functions
ctime( ), asctime( ), time

Returns
Calendar time, or -1 if not available

strftime( )

```
size_t strftime(char *s, size_t
    maxsize, const char *format,
    const struct tm *timeptr);
```
(ANSI only, not in TC, MSC, or LC; is in EC)

This function, "string format time," puts time information as formatted by format and places no more than maxsize number of characters into the string s. The formatting is similar to that used with functions such as `printf()`. Table 17 gives the most common formatting characters.

Include file

time.h

Related functions

time(), gmtime(), localtime()

Returns

Number of characters placed into `s` not including the terminating null character if the total number of characters is less than `maxsize`; otherwise, 0.

Table 17. Common String Format Characters for Time Functions

Character	Meaning
%a	abbreviated weekday name
%A	full name of the weekday
%b	abbreviated month name
%B	full name of the month
%c	locale's date and time representation
%d	day of the month (1-31)
%H	hour of the day (0-23)
%I	hour of the day (1-12)
%j	day of the year (1-366)
%m	month of the year (1-12)
%M	minute (0-59)
%p	locale's version of AM or PM
%S	seconds (0-59)
%U	week number of the year (0-53) with Sunday as the first day of the week
%w	weekday (Sunday=0 to Saturday=6)
%W	week number of the year (0-53) with Monday as the first day of the week

Character	*Meaning*
%x	locale's date representation (that is, mm/dd/yy or dd/mm/yy)
%X	locale's time representation
%y	two-digit year representation (00-99)
%Y	four-digit year representation
%Z	time zone name
%%	percent sign (%)

time( )

```
time_t time(time_t *timer);
```

The function `time()` gets the calendar time from the system; it also may assign the time to whatever `timer` points to if it is not NULL.

Include file
```
time.h
```

Related functions
```
asctime(), ctime()
```

Returns
Time as calendar time; non-ANSI forms may return the time as long values

General Utilities—stdlib.h

abort( )

```
void abort(void); (EC)
```

This function makes a program terminate because of a hardware problem or other error. Program termination can be prevented if the signal SIGABRT is processed.

Include file
stdlib.h
Functions

Related functions
atexit(), exit(), signal()

abs( )

```
int abs(int j);
```

Returns the absolute value of j.

Include file
stdlib.h

Related functions
labs()

Returns
Absolute value of j

atexit( )

```
int atexit(void (*func) (void));
(EC, LC)
```

atexit() registers the function passed as a parameter, with a minimum of 32 functions. These functions will be called at program termination.

Include file
stdlib.h

Related functions
abort(), exit, signal()

Returns
0 if registration succeeds, or a nonzero value if not

atof( )

```
double atof(const char *nptr);
```

Converts a number in the form of a string pointed to by nptr into a double-precision floating point number.

Include file
stdlib.h

Related functions
atoi(), atol()

Returns
Double-precision value after conversion; most compilers return 0 if the string is not valid

atoi( )

```
int atoi(const char *nptr);
```

Converts a string number to an integer value.

Include file
stdlib.h

Related functions
atof(), atol()

Returns
Integer value of string after conversion; most compilers return 0 if the string is not valid

atol( )

```
long int atol(const char *nptr);
```

Converts a number in the form of a string to a long integer value.

Include file
    stdlib.h

Related functions
    atof(), atoi()

Returns
    Long integer value of string after conversion; most
    compilers return 0 if the string is not valid

bsearch( )

```
void *bsearch(const void *key, const
    void *base, size_t nmemb, size_t
    size, int (*compar)(const
    void *, const void *)); (LC)
```

Provides a generic binary search routine for C. A sorted
object, such as an array, is given to the function in
base, and the routine searches for a member as
specified in key. The object is composed of nmemb
number of members, each of size size.

A comparison function is supplied by compar, which
requires two arguments. They are compared, and the
function returns an integer < 0 if the key is > *member,
0 if the key matches *member, or an integer > 0 if the
key is < *member.

Include file
    stdlib.h

Related functions
    qsort()

Returns
    void pointer to the matching member, or a NULL
    pointer if no match occurs

calloc( )

```
void *calloc(size_t nmemb,
    size_t size);
```

Creates storage on the heap for nmemb items, each of size bytes. It also sets each byte to 0.

Include file

stdlib.h -- (m)alloc.h in non-ANSI compilers

Related functions

free(), malloc(), realloc()

Returns

Void (generic) pointer for use by other functions. A NULL pointer is returned on error, such as in cases where not enough memory is available.

div( )

```
div_t div(int numer, int denom);
(EC, LC)
```

Calculates the quotient and remainder portions of numer/denom. div_t is defined in stdlib.h.

Include file

stdlib.h

Related functions

ldiv()

Returns

Quotient and remainder portions

exit( )

```
void exit(int status);
```

Causes a program to terminate due to error. Before termination, the functions previously registered by `atexit()` are called and executed in reverse order. All open streams (files) are flushed, closed, and any files created by the function `tmpfile()` are deleted.

Include file
stdlib.h

Related functions
abort(), atexit(), signal()

free( )

```
void free(void *ptr);
```

Deallocates memory that was previously allocated by `malloc()`, `calloc()`, or `realloc()`. If `ptr` is a null pointer, then no action is performed.

Include file
stdlib.h

Related functions
calloc(), malloc(), realloc()

getenv( )

```
char *getenv(const char *name);
```

Retrieves environmental information. The string returned cannot be modified by the program.

labs( )

```
long int labs(long int j); (EC)
```

Returns the absolute value of j.

ldiv( )

```
ldiv_t ldiv(long int numer,
     long int denom); (EC, LC)
```

Calculates the result of numer/denom and returns
both the quotient and remainder as the type ldiv_t.

Returns
Long integer quotient and remainder

malloc( )

```
void *malloc(size_t size);
```

It sets aside storage for an object of size `size` and returns a pointer to the beginning of that location.

Include file
stdlib.h

Related functions
calloc(), free(), realloc()

Returns
Void pointer to the block of memory, or a NULL pointer if no memory is available

mblen( )

```
int mblen(const char *s, size_t n);
```
(ANSI only, not in EC, TC, MSC, or LC)

Calculates up to `n` number of bytes in the multi-byte character pointed to by `s`.

Include file
stdlib.h

Related functions
mbtowc(), wctomb(), mbstowcs(), strlen()

Returns
If s is NULL, the function returns a nonzero value if there are state-dependent encodings, or a 0 if not. If s is

not NULL, the function returns 0 if s points to a NULL character, the number of bytes making up a valid multibyte character, or -1 if the character is not valid.

mbstowcs( )

```
size_t mbstowcs(wchar_t *pwcs,
      const char *s, size_t n);
```
(ANSI only, not in EC, TC, MSC, or LC)

Examines n multibyte characters starting with the one pointed to by s and converts them into the appropriate codes, which are then stored in pwcs. The shift state of the characters is not affected.

Include file
stdlib.h

Related functions
mblen(), wctomb(), mbtowc(), wcstombs()

Returns
-1 is returned if the character is invalid, otherwise the number of members that are converted

mbtowc( )

```
int mbtowc(wchar_t *pwc, const
      char *s, size_t n);
```
(ANSI only, not in EC, TC, MSC, or LC)

Calculates the number of bytes in the multibyte character found in s, then determines the code for its value. If the code is valid and pwc is not a null pointer, then the function places the code in pwc. No more than n characters are taken into consideration.

Include file
stdlib.h

Related functions
    mblen(), wctomb(), mbstowcs()

Returns
    If s is NULL, the function returns a nonzero value if the
    character has locale-dependent encodings, or 0 if the
    encodings are absent. If s is not NULL, the function
    returns 0 if s points to a null character, the number of
    bytes in the valid character, or -1 if the character is not
    valid.

qsort( )

```
void qsort(void *base, size_t nmemb,
     size_t size, int (*compar)
     (const void *, const void *));
```

Implements a generic "quicksort." base points to the
beginning of the object (array, etc.) to be sorted in
ascending order, which consists of nmemb members,
each of size size. The pointer compar points to a
function that compares the two pointers given as
parameters and returns an integer < 0 if the key is >
*member, 0 if the key matches *member, or an
integer > 0 if the key is < *member.

Include file
    stdlib.h

Related functions
    bsearch()

rand( )

```
int rand(void);
```

Implements a pseudo-random number generator. The
generator should first be seeded (initialized) using

srand(). Using the same seed, or without calling
srand(), rand() generates the same series of
random numbers with each call.

Include file
stdlib.h

Related functions
srand()

Returns
Integer in the range of 0 to RAND_MAX (32767).

realloc( )

```
void *realloc(void *ptr,
    size_t size);
```

Resizes to the new size size the memory set aside by a
prior call to malloc() or calloc(). The contents of
the memory are not corrupted. If space is not available
(when more is needed) at the present location, then a
new location may be selected, the contents copied there,
and a new pointer returned. ptr is a pointer to a
memory location from either malloc() or
calloc().

Include file
stdlib.h

Related functions
calloc(), free(), malloc()

Returns
void pointer to the memory just allocated, or a NULL
pointer if no memory is available

srand( )

```
void srand(unsigned int seed);
```

Initializes the pseudorandom-number generator. A different seed produces a different series of numbers.

Include file
stdlib.h

Related functions
rand()

strtod( )

```
double strtod(const char *nptr,
    char **endptr); (LC)
```

Changes a string, nptr, to a double precision value by stripping out leading whitespace characters and any invalid leading characters (valid floating-point characters include E, e, -, +, ., and the digits 0-9).

Include file
stdlib.h

Related functions
strtol(), strtoul()

Returns
Double-precision value, or 0 if problems occur

strtol( )

```
long int strtol(const char *nptr,
    char **endptr, int base);
```

Converts a string at nptr to a long integer. base is the radix of the number: if it is 0, then an octal, a decimal, or

a hexadecimal constant is expected, but other values
ranging from 2 to 36 are allowed. `endptr` is set to the
position of the first nonvalid character in the input
string.

Include file
```
stdlib.h
```

Related functions
```
strtod(), strtoul()
```

Returns
Long integer value, or 0 on error

strtoul( )

```
unsigned long int strtoul(const char
        *nptr, char **endptr, int base);
```
(EC, LC)

Converts a string at `nptr` to an unsigned long integer.
The `base` is the radix of the number; if it is 0, then an
octal, a decimal, or a hexadecimal constant is expected,
but other values ranging from 2 to 36 are allowed.
`endptr` is set to the position of the first nonvalid
character in the input string. A minus sign (–) or plus
sign (+) may not be used as part of the string.

Include file
```
stdlib.h
```

Related functions
```
strtod(), strtol()
```

Returns
Unsigned long integer value, or 0 on error

system( )

```
int system(const char *string);
```

Passes string to the host operating system or environment.

Include file

stdlib.h

Related functions

getenv()

Returns

If string is a null pointer, a nonzero value is returned *only* if a command processor is available; an implementation-defined value is returned otherwise.

wcstombs( )

```
size_t wcstombs(char *s, const
     wchar_t *pwcs, size_t n);
```
(ANSI only, not in EC, TC, MSC, or LC)

Examines no more than n multibyte characters at pwcs and stores them at s as multibyte characters in their beginning shift state.

Include file

stdlib.h

Related functions

mblen(), wctomb(), mbtowc(), mbstowcs()

Returns

If s is NULL, returns a nonzero value if the character has locale-dependent encodings, or 0 if the encodings are absent. If s is not NULL, returns 0 if s points to a null character, the number of bytes in the valid multibyte character, or -1 if the character is not valid

wctomb( )

```
int wctomb(char *s, wchar_t wchar);
```
(ANSI only, not in EC, TC, MSC, or LC)

Calculates the number of bytes required to hold the character whose code is in `wchar` and stores the multibyte character at `s`.

Include file
stdlib.h

Related functions
mblen(), mbtowc(), mbstowcs(),
wcstombs()

Returns
If `s` is NULL, the function returns a nonzero value if the character has locale-dependent encodings, or 0 if the encodings are absent. If `s` is not NULL, the function returns 0 if `s` points to a null character, the number of bytes in the valid multibyte character, or -1 if the character is not valid.

Nonlocal Jumps—setjmp.h

longjmp( )

```
void longjmp(jmp_buf env, int val);
```

Provides a means of a nonlocal jump (a jump between functions instead of within one function). `env` must be an array of type `jmp_buf` (found in `setjmp.h`) that has been initialized in a prior call to `setjmp()`. Control returns to the statement following `setjmp()`. The value `val` is returned.

Include file

```
setjmp.h
```

Related functions

```
goto(), setjmp(), signal()
```

setjmp( )

```
int setjmp(jmp_buf env);
```

Saves the environment in the array env of type jmp_buf, which is (in setjmp.h) for later use by longjmp().

Include file

```
setjmp.h
```

Related functions

```
goto(), longjmp(), signal()
```

Returns

0 if return is from a direct (initial) call, or nonzero if return is from longjmp()

Signal Handling—signal.h

raise( )

```
int raise(int sig); (EC, TC, LC)
```

Reports the signal from an error condition stored in sig.

Include file

```
signal.h
```

```
signal(), atexit(), exit(), abort()
```

0 if successful, or a nonzero value if not successful

signal( )

```
void (*signal(int sig, void
      (*func)(int)))(int);
```
(~~EC~~, ssignal() in TC)

Determines how subsequent signals are handled, based on the value of sig. If `sig = 1` (SIG_IGN), signals are ignored. If `sig = 0` (SIG_DFL), default signal-handling (defined by the implementation) is used. If `sig = -1` (SIG_ERR), the function at func is used.

Include file
```
signal.h
```

Related functions
```
raise(), atexit(), exit(), abort()
```

Returns
The previous value of func

Variable Function Arguments— stdarg.h

va_arg( )

```
type va_arg(va_list ap, type); (L̶C̶)
```

This macro deals with routines such as `printf()`, `fprintf()`, `vprintf()`, and others which have a varying number of parameters. The process is started by calling va_start(). The macro va_arg() gets the next argument in a variable parameter list and moves the pointer ahead to the next argument. The first parameters of va_arg() and va_start() should be the same. The second parameter of va_arg() is the type of the argument, such as int or double. See also vprintf().

Include file

stdarg.h

Related functions

va_end, va_start()

Returns

Next argument in the function parameter list

va_end( )

```
void va_end(va_list ap); (LC)
```

This macro causes a normal termination to reading the argument list. It *must* be called after using va_arg() for the last time, or the results may be unpredictable.

Include file

stdarg.h

Related functions

va_arg(), va_start()

va_start( )

```
void va_start(va_list ap, parmN); (LC)
```

The macro va_start() signals the beginning of the function's parameter list on the stack, which is then scanned by using va_arg() to obtain each individual argument. `va_end()` finally is called to cause a normal end to the process. The ellipsis is used in the parameter list to specify that the arguments are undetermined. At least one fixed argument should precede the ellipsis.

Include file

    stdarg.h

Related functions

    va_arg(), va_end()